ADVANCE PRAISE

"So many women wonder about their contribution to the world and are unable to articulate their purpose. The Whyography process takes the mystery out of stepping into your full purpose and soaring. So, so great!"
—Junita Flowers, Junita's Jar

"Chris Olsen's powerful Whyography process has upleveled my business significantly. By getting to my true WHY, I'm now creating more relatable content and connecting with my clients from a real, authentic and purposeful place." **—Carrie Boe, SuperStrongChick**

"Chris Olsen and the Whyography process gave me the tools to fully discover my WHY and the courage to share it with the world."
—Keri Bischoff, Keri Bischoff Consulting

"The process of learning my WHY was so revealing. I discovered things about myself that I don't know would have been uncovered without the Whyography course. Chris Olsen is an amazing coach. In my case, she worked tirelessly to get us to a place where my WHY was obvious in my story." **—Karla Heeter, Grace Gear**

CHRIS OLSEN

BUILDING A BRAND
FUELED BY PURPOSE

WHYOGRAPHY: BUILDING A BRAND FUELED BY PURPOSE

ISBN: 979-8-5689199-7-1 (First Edition)
ISBN: 979-8-9865220-6-7 (Second Edition)

Library of Congress Control Number: 2020923505

Printed in the United States of America
Third Printing: 2024

Published by Publish Her, LLC
310 1/2 Main Street South
Stillwater, Minnesota 55082
www.publishherpress.com

Illustrations by Kayla Franz

PUBLISH HER™

THE TWO MOST IMPORTANT
DAYS IN YOUR LIFE ARE THE
DAY YOU ARE BORN AND THE
DAY YOU FIND OUT WHY.

MARK TWAIN

DEDICATION

This book is dedicated to my dad. He taught me how to dance, how to be assertive, how to solve problems with creative solutions, and how to rewire an outlet. He gifted me his gap-toothed grin and his sarcastic sense of humor. He showed me the value of hard work, helping others, and taking a stand for what you believe in. He taught me that sometimes the most powerful thing you can say is nothing at all. Some days I miss him (and his homemade spaghetti sauce) more than words can say, but I am grateful to have had such a great role model in my life.

IN MEMORY OF
MARIA TOTOTZINTLE

Author's note: I first met Maria Tototzintle in 2012. For several years, we worked together producing videos for the women's economic development agency her mom once led. She was one of the most creative and talented people I've had the privilege of working with. A calm force, she never ceased to amaze me. During one video shoot in particular, after she finished filming the owner of a trapeze center, Maria decided to take a swing on a flying trapeze. I was in awe. She had the courage to climb that tiny ladder several stories up to take that giant leap. In December 2018, when I got a message from her sister Mari that Maria had been diagnosed with ovarian cancer, I was in awe of my dear friend's bravery all over again. Ten months after her diagnosis, Maria lost her battle to cancer. While nothing can fill the void in the hearts of her family and friends, her legacy lives on in all of the stories she told so beautifully over the years. She has influenced the lives of many in so many wonderful ways. This is her story.

When Maria Tototzintle was growing up, she gave a lot of thought to her career path. She saw herself working in the medical field one day. In college, she was working toward a biology major and excelling in all of her classes. But something changed along the way. She was also enjoying the art courses she was taking. She'd always been interested in visual arts and was especially passionate about sharing her view of the world through video. Maria realized she was more of an artist than a scientist. A supportive college advisor gave her the go-ahead to create a special major, and she embarked on an entirely new path to become a video producer.

Her college advisor was not Maria's only supporter. Her mother, Patti, a longtime community advocate for Latinx women and families, also happened to be the vice president of an economic development agency dedicated to supporting women and minorities when Maria was growing up. Patti not only encouraged Maria to pursue her dreams but also mentored her every step of the way.

After graduation, Maria started volunteering her time and talents to produce short videos for local nonprofits. As she was building her portfolio, she was introduced to a family friend at Minnesota's public television station who was impressed with Maria's work. She was offered a job as a production assistant. She'd be working on an educational program dedicated to empowering youth of color by encouraging them to use media to invoke discussion in the community.

Maria's role at the TV station was the springboard for her next job as an access coordinator for a nonprofit organization dedicated to helping communities develop a common understanding through media. She enjoyed her job producing video segments, providing technical assistance and teaching classes, but she was also focused on building her own video production company. She began investing in equipment and started doing freelance work on the side. In 2006, she officially launched her video production company, Tequila Digital Media.

Maria had a personal interest in promoting the local economy of Saint Paul's West Side—the vibrant and largely Latinx neighborhood where she grew up. She made connections with nonprofits focused on economic and neighborhood development and began producing videos to highlight area businesses. Those projects were instrumental in moving Maria's business plan forward. She had created a niche for herself and developed a passion for telling the stories of local entrepreneurs.

In late 2012, the nonprofit her mom once led enlisted Maria to create videos telling the stories of women business owners for its annual fundraising event. The videos debuted to an audience of more than 1,000 people and were instrumental in helping to raise hundreds of thousands of dollars in donations for the organization. For Maria, it was confirmation that she was doing the work she was always meant to do.

CONTENTS

PROLOGUE: 1

PART 1: THE STOCK...9

PART 2: THE SPICE 43

PART 3: THE SIMMER....................................73

PART 4: THE SECRET INGREDIENT.................101

PART 5: THE SAUCE....................................131

PART 6: THE SUPPER 169

PART 7: THE STORYTELLER 199

EPILOGUE 215

HOW TO USE THIS BOOK

You'll notice a pattern throughout this book—introduction, instruction, inspiration. Each section starts with a story about my personal journey. Next, there are related lessons and/or exercises to guide you in clarifying and communicating your journey. Following the lessons and/or exercises are stories from a wide range of female-identifying entrepreneurs to serve as examples.

If you intend to use this book as a guide, make your way through it at your own pace. Find a quiet place to work and carve out an hour at a time. As you work through the lessons and exercises, you'll do a fair amount of self-reflection and writing. Initially, you'll explore what makes you you, and then you'll dig into the craft of storytelling—how to put your own experiences into words, to let the world know who you are and what matters most to you. Take time to reflect and do the exercises before moving on.

If you're just here for the stories, you're in for a treat. You'll find the stories of several amazing female-identifying founders—more than 30 in total. Some of the women attended Whyography workshops and wrote these stories while learning the process shared in this book. I know you'll find them as inspiring as I do.

PROLOGUE

BASIC OR BEYONCÉ

The summer Beyoncé's single "Crazy in Love" debuted, I was working as the marketing director for a hip-hop radio station. My friend Dawn worked in advertising sales there. Some of her clients were nightclubs that partnered with the radio station to host parties with DJs, cheap drinks, dance contests and prizes. Dawn and I attended many of the club events together. Our role was to make sure everything went off without a hitch. Sometimes that meant sampling the drink specials while debating whether Destiny's Child would make it without Beyoncé and sweating our asses off on the dance floor. We took our jobs very seriously.

During that time, Dawn was keeping an eye out for her future husband. I had no marriage plans, but I paid close attention to Dawn's vetting process, thinking I might learn something. It almost always went down the same way. A couple of guys would approach us. They'd become entranced by Dawn's height and beauty (she's taller than 6 feet with giant blue eyes). They'd inevitably ask the same three questions: "How tall are you?" "Are you single?" "Can I buy you a drink?" Dawn would suggest we'd both like a drink and then she'd ask one question of her potential suitors: "What do you do for a living?"

I admired Dawn's directness. I almost never asked that question of someone I'd just met. Not at a nightclub or a dinner party or even a professional networking event. As I sipped my drink and strained to hear the responses, I realized the men were pitching themselves to Dawn like they were being interviewed for a job—rattling off qualifications as if reciting the glossed-up bullet points from their business bios. During that

"Crazy in Love" summer, I watched dozens of men make their pitches to Dawn.

The responses weren't all that surprising. As young professionals entering the job market, we start creating a "story" for ourselves based on what we think the "right people" will want to hear. It begins by sharing academic achievements—test scores, grade point average, class ranking, number of college admission offers. It continues as a resume or business bio with employment dates and job titles. We share that story over and over again, adjusting as needed to impress a potential school, employer, partner, etc. Here's the problem: The basic business bio is not your story at all.

Business bios have been used to tout professional qualifications for centuries. Leonardo da Vinci created a business bio more than 500 years ago hoping to secure a gig with the soon-to-be Duke of Milan. In the 1950s the basic business bio was formalized and became an expectation of employers. It was digitized in the early 2000s when platforms like Monster, CareerBuilder and LinkedIn launched. But the structure of the basic business bio has changed very little in 70 years.

Take a look at your LinkedIn profile. It's the epitome of a basic business bio. It highlights all the basics—your education, the jobs you've held, perhaps a few glowing recommendations. It barely scratches the surface of what makes you uniquely you. Think about times you've scrolled through the LinkedIn profile of someone you've never met. After reading it, was there something that made you feel a genuine connection with that person? Did you gain a solid understanding of their values, what they stand for, or the difference they're making in the world? A LinkedIn profile is beneficial in many ways. And glossy bullet points provide some insight about the person behind the profile. But a basic business bio is focused on your WHAT and not your WHY.

WHY YOUR WHY MATTERS

Your WHY is your purpose, your values in action, your North Star. We all have a WHY. We are all meant for something bigger than ourselves.

It's not always evident, but there are signs throughout our lives that lead to it.

Getting clear on your WHY is like discovering your internal compass. It helps ensure you know which way is north, even when the skies are dark and cloudy and the stars and horizon are nowhere in sight. When you're off track, your WHY points you in the right direction. It restores hope. It's the fuel that keeps you moving forward. Clarifying your WHY empowers you to pursue your purpose, to live your WHY and to honor your calling.

Living your WHY is good for you. Humans do better when we do better. Research shows that pursuing purpose leads to better sleep, better overall health, better quality of life and a longer life. As it turns out, it's good for business too. The king of WHY, Simon Sinek, is known for his quote "People don't buy WHAT you do, they buy WHY you do it." In other words, leading with your WHY in business sets you up for success.

While the basic business bio is living in the past, the way business is conducted has evolved considerably. There's no longer a clear delineation between for-profit companies where cash is king and nonprofit organizations that solve society's complex problems. Today's consumers expect businesses to do the right thing, to put people and the planet first. This is especially true for the largest living generation in the U.S.—millennials. More than ever, they're using their dollars to make a difference. Along with the majority of all consumers, they're committed to supporting and recommending businesses that are aligned with their values and boycotting brands that aren't.

All that consumer support means purpose-driven businesses perform better. In fact, they outperform the stock market and yield a greater return on investment. That means investors are more likely to back entrepreneurs and businesses that clearly and confidently communicate their purpose and impact. When you lead with WHY in your business, it also connects you with employees who share your values and believe in your mission. Employees of purpose-driven businesses are twice as engaged and satisfied with their work. They're more likely to stick around and succeed within companies that stand for something they believe in.

They become your business's biggest cheerleaders and your brand's most loyal advocates.

WOMEN AND WHY

Leading with your WHY is especially important for female-identifying business founders. Sexism is alive and kicking in 21st-century America. Up until the 1990s, women in the U.S. couldn't legally get a business loan without a male cosigner—a throwback to colonial law that stripped an entire gender of its legal identity. A female's identity was covered under her father's at birth and then her husband's upon marriage, which meant she couldn't legally own or work in a business. While many laws have changed, their influence continues to affect the lives of women in numerous ways.

Women face significant hurdles in launching and growing small businesses. There are around 13 million women-owned businesses in the United States today. Those businesses generate close to $2 trillion in annual revenue and employ more than 9 million people. Despite their significant contributions to society and the economy, female founders receive less than a quarter of small-business bank loans and a tiny fraction (less than 3 percent) of venture capital. Those numbers decrease exponentially for women of color. Women who do receive business funding are more likely to receive smaller amounts and higher interest rates than men.

Gender bias plays a significant role in access to business resources. While there have been shifts in perceptions about women's' leadership and business capacity over the past few decades, broad-ranging societal changes take time. Nevertheless, there is something you can do to set yourself up for success, and it need not wait until the patriarchy has been dismantled. This critical shift is one you have the power to make happen and quickly: Change the way you talk about your business. Stop leading with your WHAT and start leading with your WHY.

It's common for female-identifying founders to struggle when pitching their business, and not just to funders. As a business owner, you must be comfortable and confident when presenting yourself to everyone. This is not an issue for most men. They easily breeze through their laundry list of credentials. They confidently state business projections and outcomes. Women are often hesitant to share information. We're more likely to compare our scorecards to others and minimize our success and superpowers. The result is that we receive fewer resources and opportunities to ensure our businesses survive and thrive.

THE POWER OF PURPOSE AND STORYTELLING

Beyoncé is a badass, chart-busting, ceiling-smashing wonder woman. Even if you're not a fan, you have to admit she's a force to be reckoned with. Not long ago, I came across an article titled "Beyoncé and Her Brand" that provided a rundown of her stats. It was an impressive list, but even so, I don't recall her net worth or how much money her tours or Coachella performance raked in. I don't remember the number of awards she'd won. I'm pretty sure her Instagram followers are in the millions, but I don't know if it's tens of millions or hundreds of millions. I don't recall how many of her songs made it to the top of the Billboard charts, though I'm almost positive "Crazy in Love" was one of them.

The thing about the article is that it was exactly like a basic business bio—all stats and no story. If the glossy bullet points of a megastar who's clearly in a league of her own are difficult to recall, odds are stats and credentials are not what will resonate with your audience either.

One of the most powerful ways to communicate is through storytelling. Stories engage audiences, influence decisions, inspire communities and ignite action. Stories build bridges to the past and the future. They link us together and remind us that we're not alone in the world. Storytelling is an especially powerful tool for amplifying the voices of those who've been marginalized. The voices of women—and particularly women of color—are underrepresented everywhere, but especially in business. Your story is important. It needs to be heard. No one else on the planet has a story exactly like yours.

A Whyography is the Beyoncé of biographies. It combines the

principles of storytelling and the power of purpose to do what a basic bio can't. It honors your journey and what it took to get where you are today. It articulates your values, the problems you're solving and the difference you're making in the world. It attracts customers, supporters and employees who not only align with your values, but who revere your brand and their connection to it. A Whyography, and the process of developing it, gives you the confidence to share your story with the world and lead with your WHY.

Are you satisfied using a decades-old basic business bio to show the world WHAT you do—or are you ready to connect with an audience that cares about WHY you're doing it? Are you content serving customers who are driven by consuming commodified goods and services—or are you ready to build a community that respects your approach and rallies around your mission? Are you comfortable with the status quo—or are you ready to get the resources and opportunities you deserve? You get to decide. Would you rather be basic? Or Beyoncé?

PART 1:
THE STOCK

HIDE THE DAMN GUN

It was summer's end in Minnesota, which meant 80-degree days and temps dipping into the 50s after sunset. On this particular night, I was alone, navigating the crowded streets of downtown Minneapolis in a black Cadillac Escalade that featured larger-than-life graphics of Destiny's Child along with the logo of the hip-hop radio station where I worked as the director of marketing. It had huge 22-inch sparkling chrome rims and a state-of-the-art sound system with woofers so big the booming bass made my teeth vibrate.

My often surly yet entirely devoted promotions team of late teen and early 20s radio announcer wannabes loved driving that vehicle. I was nearly a decade older than most of them, and that truck came with more attention than I was comfortable with. It also sacked all chances of arriving anywhere discreetly. That evening, I wished I was doing what I had imagined a person with my job would be doing—meeting Prince for an acoustic performance and low-key gab session at Paisley Park.

Instead, I was alone in an alleyway behind a popular nightclub looking for the host of a music TV channel reality program dedicated to extreme makeovers on crappy cars—a rapper I'll call "Z." I spotted his stretch limo and parked nearby.

At 5 feet 2 inches tall, the leap down from the Escalade was an ordeal for me, and that evening I practically rolled an ankle. I steadied myself on my chunky Steve Madden wedge sandals, straightened my distressed jean jacket, adjusted my leather shoulder bag and did my best to look like I had my shit together. I thought about checking my reflection in the side window—I'd had my hair done earlier that week—

but I knew I was being watched and opted not to. Just then someone from the rapper/TV host's crew approached me.

"Hi, I'm Chris!" I said cheerfully, with my hand outstretched.

He quickly shook it without introducing himself. "We've got a problem," he grumbled. "Security won't let us in and we're about to leave."

"Oh no, you're all good," I chirped, pretending not to be worried. "Hold tight and let me see what's up."

I grabbed my fluorescent pink clipboard and approached the shadow of a muscle-bound security guard dressed entirely in black, standing at the dimly lit back entrance of the club.

"Hi there! Z's management is saying they couldn't get in," I said in the most upbeat of tones. "Is there a problem?"

He grunted something that was inaudible while simultaneously opening the door for me. A sweltering mix of sweat and club music hit me in the face. The venue was packed, and the crowd was bouncing in unison to a familiar hip-hop anthem. Just inside, next to the metal detector, the club's manager stood dressed in a crisp dark suit and signaled me to come closer. As I began to ask him what was going on, his lips were already moving, saying something that I could barely make out.

"What?!" I shouted. Instead of speaking louder, he got closer.

"No. Guns. In. The. Club," he said slowly. His lips brushed lightly against my ear.

I paused and stepped back. It was not what I expected to hear. My adrenaline started to rush, and my palms began to sweat. Though I wanted the look on my face to say, "I am well aware of the club's no-gun policy," I'm sure it was more like that of an overly expressive and awkward teenage girl who had just learned about a cool kid's party that everyone at school had been invited to but her.

"Who's got a gun?" I squeaked.

The club manager didn't hear my impression of Bobby Brady going through puberty. He did manage to read my lips and nodded in the direction of the limo.

"Oh. OK. I'll take care of it," I said with all the confidence I could muster.

I'd dealt with a lot of unexpected and unbelievable incidents during music shows at nightclubs. Relentless fans. Bar brawls. Performers' crazy late-night requests for fast food. But never a gun. I had no idea what "taking care of it" meant. What I did know was that it was after 11 p.m. and if Z didn't perform soon, there was a good chance the amped-up crowd would become unruly.

I walked back toward the limo where Z and his team were standing. "No guns in the club," I said to his manager, annoyed that he had neglected to mention the gun earlier. My teeth began to chatter so I clenched my jaw tightly and flashed the kind of permanent grin you might see formed into the face of a Ken doll.

"These guys are from Cali," the manager said, adding something about a permit to conceal and carry.

Until then, I hadn't considered the impact of the whole East Coast–West Coast hip-hop rivalry. Perhaps because it had taken place a decade earlier and we were in Minnesota, smack-dab in the middle of both coasts. Now I wondered if it was the reason for the manager's nonchalant tone.

"Will you take care of the gun?" Z asked politely.

I had worked with hundreds of famous people during my 10 years in radio, but I had never been fazed by their status. I hadn't asked for a single autograph, and I rarely lined up with the rest of the staff and interns for photos. I treated celebrities like regular people because they mostly just seemed like regular people to me. For one fleeting moment, I actually considered tucking the gun into the small Coach bag that was draped over my shoulder.

I quickly snapped back to reality and explained that since I was responsible for managing the event, I wouldn't be useful hanging around in an alley with a loaded weapon. He seemed to understand. There was talk among his team about whether they should leave without doing the show, and a guy who worked for the record label was trying to convince them Z needed to go on as planned.

I went back to the Escalade and called my boss, the radio station's general manager. He was a tightly wound guy in his late 50s or early 60s who had spent the majority of his career as a sales manager for the local sports radio station. He landed at the market's brand-new hip-hop radio station after being unceremoniously pushed out of his last job.

He didn't answer the phone the first time. I was sure he was asleep, so I kept calling until he picked up. He was groggy and agitated as I explained what was going on. When I asked him what he wanted me to do, he suggested I take the gun and put it in the limo.

"Are you out of your mind?!" I squawked. My filter, which was typically in place for addressing figures of authority with respect, had disappeared. "Do you think it's OK for me to be handling a gun?"

"I don't know what to tell you," he responded tersely. "We need the revenue from this event." After a brief pause, he added, "Just hide the damn gun!"

I was pissed. It wasn't the first time I'd observed profit prioritized over people in the radio industry. In some ways, I'd become numb to it. Revenue was at stake. There were budgets that had been dictated by the corporate office, and I was expected to do whatever it took to ensure the radio station made money that night. I had a job to do. I needed to shift into problem-solving mode and make this show happen. Without another word, I hung up the phone and cursed under my breath as I walked back toward the limo.

I was furious with my boss. I was frustrated with Z's management for threatening to back out of a contractual obligation to perform because the venue didn't allow weapons on the premises. When I approached them and began to speak, my words were clipped.

"Here's what's going to happen," I asserted. "Someone from the record company is going to stay out here with the gun, and the rest of us are going inside. Z is going onstage in 15 minutes."

With that, I spun on my heels and marched toward the club's entrance. I hoped no one noticed as I wobbled on my wedges like a clumsy newborn foal, but it would have been hard to miss. Especially since I flung my arm out—neon pink clipboard in hand—to steady myself.

Having grown up with brothers who teased me relentlessly about my klutziness, I expected someone to make a joke as I fast-walked toward the door. There were no guffaws—only the sound of feet shuffling on gritty pavement. Not another word was spoken as we entered the club. Within minutes, the performance was underway.

THE SMOKING GUN

The day after the Z performance, standing just outside the radio station sales manager's office, I handed him a zipper pouch filled with the proceeds from the event. This was customary. I'd stay at the venue after closing with the club's manager and count the stacks of cash from door admissions. Then I'd jump back into the Escalade with thousands of dollars, drive home, sleep a few hours and head into the radio station.

On any other day, as I turned in the cash from a show, I would've played along with the sales manager's giddy excitement as he asked, "How'd we do?" I would have felt a strange sense of pride about producing a successful event and doing my part to help meet the radio station's revenue goals.

That day was different. I hadn't gotten any sleep. The phone call with my boss the night before was playing on a nonstop loop in my head. All I could think was, "No one gives a shit about me; they only care about the money." My boss, the sales manager, the finance manager—most of the management team—rarely came to events. They hadn't dealt with crazy crowds or ducked into a back room to avoid being caught up in a bar fight. The risk of having employees transport large sums of cash during the wee hours of the morning didn't seem to concern them. And they couldn't be bothered with something like how to handle a loaded gun at a radio station event.

The sales manager peered into the pouch and fished out the receipt that was wrapped up with the bills.

"That's it?" he asked before I had a chance to utter a word. He was clearly disappointed by what he saw. "How many people were there?"

This particular sales manager was one of the nicest people I'd worked with in my entire radio career. He meant well and he genuinely cared about people. But he was, when all was said and done, the money guy. And in that moment, he was completely unaware of how upset I was or that my eyes were welling up with tears.

"Are you serious?" I asked. My voice cracked, and my cheeks and neck turned red with heat.

"Seems like the number should be bigger," he added, still oblivious to my reaction.

"Are you kidding me?!" I shouted, snapping him out of his fixation on the pouch of money. "The show almost didn't happen because Z had a loaded gun and the club wouldn't let him in!"

A look of panic flashed over his face. "I didn't know," he gulped.

"That's just it! Nobody knows! Nobody fucking cares!" I said.

I marched into my office, slamming the door behind me. I sank into my chair and began to sob. I felt utterly defeated. Almost immediately, I began to worry if I'd be fired for swearing at the sales manager. I thought about how empowering it would be to walk out the front door of that radio station without looking back. I wondered if anyone would even notice.

That night I called my dad. I couldn't muster up the courage to tell him about the incident with the gun because I was afraid of what he might say. He wasn't anti-gun. He owned two that I knew about—a pistol he kept in a wooden box on a high shelf in his dining room closet and a shotgun he used for hunting, which was stored somewhere I wasn't privy to. I'd only seen it in photos of goose hunting trips he'd taken to Canada. When we were growing up, he told my siblings and me not to touch the pistol in the closet. I never did.

I also decided not to tell my dad about my breakdown at the office. I suspected he'd say something about my emotions getting the best of me. The piece of advice I'd heard most from him over the years: "Sometimes the most powerful thing you can say is nothing at all." This meant many things. First and foremost, actions speak louder than words. And also, don't say the first thing that comes to mind in every tough situation. Take a breath. Give yourself time to process. Respond rather than react.

Instead of focusing on the fact that I was dealing with a major misalignment of values with my employer, I focused on a single issue— the one problem that didn't feel insurmountable.

"It freaks me out to be transporting thousands of dollars in cash like that," I said.

"Then don't do it," he said.

He had a knack for cutting to the chase and was never one to mince words. We'd had the conversation before, and it was clear he didn't have the patience to have it again. I attempted to drag it out by asking what he meant by "don't do it," but he said I already knew the answer. He said he had to get off the phone—he was in the middle of cooking a pot of his homemade spaghetti sauce.

I wish I could say I had a productive meeting with my boss the next day, that I stood up for myself and what I thought was right, and that he was willing to address the tough stuff within the organization. That's not what happened. Whenever there seemed to be an opportunity to have a conversation, he shut me down. "I'm sorry, I don't have time," he said. He was waiting for an important phone call, or on his way to a meeting, or just about to head out for the day.

What did I do? I stewed for a while. Then I did what a lot of people who are in denial about a situation that's not right for them do—I maintained the status quo. I hoped things would magically get better. I pushed down my realization that my job and the company I was working for were wrong for me. I did my best to achieve success within a wildly dysfunctional work environment. That is, until my position was eliminated a couple of years later.

SPEAK TRUTH ... EVEN WHEN IT'S UNCOMFORTABLE.

KAMALA HARRIS

INSTRUCTION

UPBRINGING AND VALUES

Growing up, nightly sit-down suppers were the norm for my family. My dad worked two jobs, which meant he rarely cooked, but when he did, it was kind of a big deal. His specialty dish was spaghetti with made-from-scratch red sauce. He spent hours doing the prep to create the stock—chopping, mincing and crushing vegetables.

Though we were a family of six, he'd use an 80-quart pot to make his sauce, which was enough to feed a small army. He loved having an audience in the kitchen and would often mimic Julia Child, whose cooking show we watched on PBS. Each time he began making a batch, he'd say with his best Julia impression, "Every great sauce starts with a solid foundation."

Just as the stock was the foundation for my dad's sauce, your upbringing and values are the base for your Whyography. No matter who you are or how far you've come, your upbringing and values play a part in the choices you make every day. They impact your decisions about relationships, work and the direction your life takes. They are influenced by many different people, experiences and events throughout your lifetime.

Oftentimes as children, we internalize our parents' values and they stick with us through adulthood. Sometimes we reject the values of our upbringing. Other times we adopt values that are dominant in society. It's important to understand the values that were instilled as you were growing up and those that became an important part of who you are as an adult. Think about what exactly you value today and why you hold those values.

Just as your values are central to who you are, they are part of your company's DNA. They help keep you moving forward no matter what—through the ups and downs and every twist and turn. Exploring your upbringing and values is essential to building your Whyography. Getting clarity around what you stand for will help you better articulate it to your audience.

EXERCISE: YOUR UPBRINGING

This writing exercise is intended to help you mine your past for important details, identify what is most relevant to your story and get your creative juices flowing. Answer each of the questions as quickly as possible. As you recall your memories, focus on what comes to mind first.

1. When and where were you born?
2. How many siblings did you have and what was your birth order? Did it change over time? What was it like being the oldest/middle/ youngest kid in your family?
3. How many places did you live as a child and what do you remember about living there?
4. Who was your predominant parental figure and why?
5. What was your fondest childhood memory and what was your age at the time?
6. What childhood memory would you change if you could and what was your age at the time?
7. What was your favorite family tradition?
8. Was there a family tradition you dreaded?
9. What was a moment when you realized your family's social class or noticed that you had more or less than others? What was your age at the time?
10. What was a moment when you realized your family's religious affiliation or spiritual beliefs? What did it mean to you and what was your age at the time?
11. What was a moment when you realized your family's political affiliation? What did it mean to you and what was your age at the time?
12. What were the values that were important to your parents/family as you were growing up (even those that may not be consistent with your values today)?

EXERCISE: YOUR VALUES

In this exercise, select all of the personal values that reflect who you are today. Work quickly; go with your gut and don't spend too much time overanalyzing. List additional values that are important to you that you don't see here. Once you've completed the exercise, take some time to consider which of your values were the result of your upbringing, which you adopted later in life and why.

Acceptance	Community	Endurance
Accomplishment	Compassion	Energy
Accountability	Competence	Enjoyment
Accuracy	Concentration	Enthusiasm
Achievement	Confidence	Equality
Adaptability	Connection	Ethicalness
Alertness	Consciousness	Excellence
Altruism	Consistency	Exploration
Ambition	Contentment	Expression
Amusement	Contribution	Fairness
Assertiveness	Control	Fame
Attentiveness	Conviction	Family
Awareness	Cooperation	Fearlessness
Balance	Courage	Feelings
Beauty	Courtesy	Fidelity
Boldness	Creativity	Focus
Bravery	Credibility	Fortitude
Brilliance	Curiosity	Freedom
Calmness	Decisiveness	Friendship
Candor	Dedication	Frugality
Capability	Dependability	Fun
Carefulness	Determination	Generosity
Certainty	Devotion	Giving
Challenge	Dignity	Goodness
Charity	Discipline	Grace
Clarity	Discovery	Gratitude
Cleanliness	Drive	Greatness
Collaboration	Effectiveness	Growth
Comfort	Efficiency	Harmony
Commitment	Empathy	Health
Communication	Empowerment	Honesty

Honor
Hope
Humility
Humor
Imagination
Independence
Individuality
Innovation
Insightfulness
Inspiration
Integrity
Intelligence
Intensity
Intuition
Irreverence
Joy
Justice
Kindness
Knowledge
Leadership
Learning
Liberty
Logic
Love
Loyalty
Mastery
Maturity
Moderation
Motivation
Openness
Optimism
Order
Organization
Originality
Passion
Patience
Peace
Performance
Persistence
Playfulness
Poise
Potential

Power
Presence
Productivity
Professionalism
Prosperity
Purpose
Quality
Rationalism
Reason
Recognition
Recreation
Reflection
Resourcefulness
Respect
Responsibility
Restraint
Results
Reverence
Rigor
Riskiness
Satisfaction
Security
Self-reliance
Selflessness
Sensitivity
Serenity
Service
Sharing
Silence
Simplicity
Sincerity
Skillfulness
Solitude
Spirituality
Spontaneity
Stability
Status
Stewardship
Strength
Structure
Success
Supportiveness

Sustainability
Talent
Teamwork
Temperance
Thankfulness
Thoroughness
Thoughtfulness
Timeliness
Tolerance
Toughness
Tradition
Tranquility
Transparency
Trust
Trustworthiness
Understanding
Uniqueness
Unity
Valor
Victory
Vigor
Vision
Vitality
Wealth
Winningness
Wisdom
Wonder

EXERCISE: YOUR VALUES IN ACTION TRACKER

This exercise is designed to help you narrow down your top values. Doing so can be tricky—you may find yourself focusing on values that are aspirational, rather than those that show up in your day-to-day life. One way to zero in on values that are central to who you are today is to look at the decisions you make about where you allocate your time, money and expertise—and, specifically, the companies and causes you choose to devote your resources to. Create your Values in Action Tracker using the example as your guide.

EXAMPLE:

BRAND, BUSINESS OR ORGANIZATION	SUPPORT, OPPOSE OR CONFLICTED	RATIONALE	VALUES
Walmart	Oppose	• Treats employees poorly • Destroys small businesses • Peddles fast fashion and low-quality products	• Fairness • Community • Quality • Responsibility • Accountability
Nike	Conflicted	• Treats women in the company poorly • Provides unsafe and unhealthy conditions for factory workers • Creates ad campaigns elevating community support to divert attention from internal issues	• Fairness • Equality • Diversity • Integrity • Responsibility
Beautycounter	Support	• Makes nontoxic beauty products • Lobbies to change beauty industry standards • Empowers women	• Transparency • Integrity • Equality • Health • Sustainability

Spend a few minutes thinking about three or four companies or causes you have made a conscious decision not to support. Perhaps you don't like the quality of the products or have had a bad customer service experience. Maybe the company or founder have political or religious affiliations that aren't in line with your views. Also consider brands you feel conflicted about supporting. Perhaps you don't agree with the company's philosophies or practices, but you purchase their products anyway, because they give back in some way, or they're affordable, convenient or delicious—but you feel regretful about it. On the tracker, list each brand, whether you oppose or feel conflicted about it, your rationale, and your personal values that conflict with the brand.

Next, think about three or four companies or causes you're passionate about supporting and why. Consider the kind of car you drive, the clothing labels in your closet, the beauty brands you use, the food brands you consume, and why you choose those brands. Reflect on brands you consistently recommend to others and companies you revere because they support causes that are important to you. List each brand on the Values in Action Tracker, note that you support it, your reasons for doing so, and your personal values that align with that brand. If specific brands don't come to mind, list organizations you support by donating money or volunteering your time.

As you reflect on values that conflict with or align with a particular brand, review your selections from the list in the previous values exercise and add more as needed.

EXERCISE: YOUR VALUES (TOP 5)

Now that you've identified some of the ways your values show up in your daily life, it's time to narrow your values list down to your top five. Start by eliminating any that you don't feel 100 percent connected to. Next, group similar values together. For example, collaboration, teamwork, harmony and unity are similar values that could be grouped together. Choose the value you feel most connected to in each group. After you've narrowed your list to five, consider whether each was the result of your upbringing or adopted later and write down details.

EXAMPLE:

Integrity. This is a value I learned from my dad. His motto was "say what you do and do what you say." He didn't just talk the talk; he walked the walk. Throughout my life, I witnessed him doing the right thing, even when it wasn't easy or took more time, effort or resources. He taught me the value of working hard, helping others and taking a stand for what you believe in.

INSPIRATION

KATIE STELLER
STELLER HAIR COMPANY

As 18-year-old Katie Steller was wheeled into the operating room, a million thoughts went through her mind. Growing up with an autoimmune disease was far from easy. She dealt with issues most kids her age couldn't imagine, including medical procedures that forced her to drop out of school—twice. Now, having her colon removed was Katie's best shot at getting better. It came with mixed emotions. While the surgery was expected to improve her life, it would bring a new set of challenges.

Katie found herself thinking back to an event that took place in the weeks before her surgery, an event many people take for granted—a day at the salon. Her hair had begun to fall out, and her mom treated her to some TLC with a professional stylist. On that day, Katie felt cared for in a way that transformed her inside and out.

After surgery, Katie thought about her future in a new way. She decided to pursue a career as a hairstylist, and she felt driven to explore small business ownership. She trained at the acclaimed Aveda Institute in Minneapolis, Minnesota, took a job at a salon to learn the ropes, and then worked as an instructor. All while hatching a plan to build a different kind of salon. Katie's vision: focus on people first. Pay a living wage. Offer training and benefits rare to the industry. Provide a flexible work environment. Create an inclusive community. And above all, be kind.

At 22, Katie realized her dream. She launched Steller Hair Company as a five-chair salon in Northeast Minneapolis. A true entrepreneur, Katie continued to grow, adding chairs and staff and imagining what was next. She also started a nonprofit, Steller Kindness Project, to recognize individuals who are making a difference in the world through acts of kindness. She hopes to inspire others to be kind as well. She and her kindness squad head out into the community regularly, offering complimentary haircuts and care packages to those in need.

Katie has received numerous awards for her workplace practices, including the Minnesota Young Entrepreneur of the Year Award from the U.S. Small Business Administration in 2018. That same year, through the Steller Kindness Project, she received something even better: the privilege of gifting a compassionate salon experience to a 12-year-old girl with similar medical issues to her own.

In late 2018, Katie celebrated another milestone when she opened the newly expanded Steller Hair Company with 10 chairs and her dream team. She kept her former salon space for training and special events like a Kindness Boutique, which offered thousands of gently used clothing items to single moms for free. It was the first of many community events Katie has hosted.

Over the years, Steller Hair Company has become much more than a salon. Ask Katie why it exists, and she'll tell you: "To do the most good that my heart and hands can accomplish in this short and uncertain life."

SHAWNTAN HOWELL
GIRLS ARE POWERFUL

Like many tweens and teens, Shawntan Howell wrestled with body image issues. She was taller than most of the girls in her class and remembers what it was like to ride in the back seat of a compact car, knees pressed into the seat ahead of her. As the person in front of her grumbled, and Shawntan tried to reposition her legs, she thought, "I just don't fit." The feeling that she didn't fit was pervasive at times, but as she grew older, Shawntan learned to overcome negative thoughts about herself by using positive self-talk.

Then her young daughter, Jalyn, began to struggle with the same issues. Seeing Jalyn doubt herself was heartbreaking for Shawntan, and her motherly instincts kicked in. She wanted all girls to know their worth. So she printed messages of empowerment on T-shirts and wore them every chance she got—becoming a walking billboard for the cause. Not only did her daughter take notice, but others did too. An IT project manager by day and an entrepreneur at heart, Shawntan was inspired to start a parttime business and launched a line of apparel and accessories with her "Girls Are Powerful" messaging.

Shawntan sought guidance to grow her business concept and was told there just wasn't a market for the apparel she had created. She was determined to find a way to carry out her mission to help girls. She began speaking at community events and launched Girls Are Powerful as an organization dedicated to helping girls and young women build self-esteem.

Then something happened that shook her own confidence. Shawntan was laid off from the corporate job she'd held for a decade. When she was feeling her lowest and struggling to get out of bed, a local organization invited her to do a speaking gig. Shawntan knew she had to pull herself together. She had to believe in herself and her vision for the organization—not just to show herself, but to show all the girls she worked with what owning your power looked like.

Over the next year, Shawntan took the opportunity to work on Girls Are Powerful full time. She got busy developing and delivering outreach programs for girls, providing them with tools to see and believe they are powerful, beautiful, smart, confident, unique and determined (what Shawntan calls "power words"). She began partnering with groups and organizations passionate about helping to deliver her message. As her programs gained momentum, she started receiving support from companies that appreciated the Girls Are Powerful mission, like the Ann Bancroft Foundation, Minnesota Timberwolves, Target and Wells Fargo.

Today, Girls Are Powerful has created a growing community of empowered girls through educational workshops and special events. Shawntan imagines a future where all those confident girls grow into powerful women who are changing the world. And she is living proof that when you own your power, amazing things can happen.

JORDYN DIORIO POLSKI
MEND JEWELRY

Jordyn DiOrio Polski was in the mood to break something. More specifically, she wanted to smash apart some old costume jewelry. It wasn't that she had anything against the baubles—she'd always loved jewelry and accessories. She had started wearing a wristwatch at age 4, before she could even tell time. But she was missing her grandmother, who had passed away a few years earlier. The loss had been difficult for Jordyn, but transforming vintage jewelry into something that captured the timeless essence of her grandma made her feel close to her, and it was cathartic. So she kept deconstructing the old pieces and creating new jewelry designs.

Although the process was therapeutic, Jordyn didn't see making jewelry as anything other than a hobby. Her long-term goal was to own a business someday, but she wasn't sure what exactly it would be. Then, as she rang in 2017, she experienced a major shift. The pull of entrepreneurship had gotten stronger. "Why not make jewelry my business?" she thought.

Jordyn started by refining her jewelry designs. She especially enjoyed working with precious gemstones and believed each held a specific kind of energy. She began to envision a line of necklaces that were classic, beautiful and simple, made from stones known to promote positive and healing energy. Jewelry had been a source of positive energy for Jordyn, and now her designs could do the same for others. She enlisted the help of her sister Julie—a color consultant with design expertise—on her branding.

Just four weeks into the new year, Jordyn launched MEND Jewelry. She created a business plan, formed an LLC, opened a business banking account, launched a website, and began selling her new creations online and at special events and pop-up shops. There was a significant change in the way she talked about designing jewelry. It was no longer a hobby; it was a legitimate business.

Jordyn told everyone she encountered about her business. A friend who'd purchased a necklace told Jordyn about someone who admired the piece and wanted to meet her—Katherine Forrester Schneewind, owner of Forrester Wealth Management. Katherine was inspired by Jordyn's story and spirit, and her long-term goal was to invest in a female entrepreneur. After meeting with Jordyn, she and her husband decided to invest in MEND. That investment enabled Jordyn to focus on growing the business, which was exactly what she needed.

She's achieved some significant milestones for MEND, including selling her products online at Nordstrom and winning New York Now's Best New Product award. Jordyn believes her greater purpose is to help women feel empowered the way Katherine and others have done for her. Whether it's manifesting the positive energy of the stones in her jewelry designs or pursuing a longtime goal to launch a business, she wants to inspire others to let go of their fears and follow their passion.

LAURA BOYD
LEADERSHIP DELTA

Laura Boyd was distracted. Watching her son participate in his confirmation ceremony filled her heart with joy. But now, as she observed the eighth graders at the front of the church, she became fixated on how they were behaving. The boys were muddling their way through the ceremony, joking and elbowing one another. The girls were well prepared and confidently gave their testimonies. It was the exact opposite of what she'd observed with a group of recent female college graduates she'd been meeting with about career aspirations. Around the time young women's confidence was starting to waver, young men were beginning to lead with theirs.

Laura had always been intrigued by human behavior. She navigated a difficult upbringing with a father who struggled with addiction. Her family moved 18 times before she was 12 years old. As she got older, she realized her path could go one of two ways: She could become a stereotype and repeat her father's cycle of dysfunction, or she could live by her mother's example of strength and endurance and make a better life for herself. Laura chose the latter. She majored in psychology and earned a master's degree in organizational leadership. She worked in high-level marketing positions. In 2006, she became a shareholder for a Minneapolis, Minnesota-based marketing and communications firm. As president of the firm, Laura experienced firsthand the power of coaching teams.

While watching the kids at church that day, Laura finally understood her true calling: to empower emerging leaders. Not just as part of her job, but as her whole job. She initially considered working for a major corporation because she knew they invested heavily in developing internal talent. Ultimately, Laura realized she could have greater influence on leaders and teams as an outside consultant providing a fresh perspective on organizational challenges. That's when Leadership Delta was born.

Whether it's the succession or onboarding of a CEO or other leadership, the transition of key team members, a company merger or acquisition, a rebrand or major communication shift—Leadership Delta works with organizations to navigate what Laura calls a "change event." She and her team assess the organization's current reality and map out a plan to achieve their desired outcomes.

Laura's area of specialty is supporting female leaders. She's worked hard to understand the factors that cause women to doubt themselves and their abilities. She coaches them on overcoming imposter syndrome, shifting their mindset and the stories they tell themselves, and ultimately becoming more confident leaders. It's the part of her work Laura finds most fulfilling.

For Laura, the leap to entrepreneurship was the perfect path for her to fully combine her purpose and her profession. She has a passion for supporting others who are pursuing their purpose and also shares her experiences through public speaking.

SUSIE MOSCHKAU
FLIP'EM THE BIRD

Susie Moschkau was binge-watching "Game of Thrones." As the unwatched episodes dwindled down, an uneasy feeling crept in. She wondered what she'd watch next, but she also wondered what she would do next—with her life. She was 39 years old, a wife, a mom of three and a corporate marketing maven with an MBA. And she had just been laid off for the second time in two years due to downsizing. Then, Susie stumbled upon a commencement speech given by comedian Jim Carrey. His dad had wanted to be a comedian but took an accountant job instead. He was laid off when Jim was 12. "You can fail at what you don't want," he said. "So you might as well take a chance at doing what you love."

When Susie was a kid and thinking about a career path, she was drawn to the safer route. She grew up in a family of small-business owners. While there were many great things about it, she also saw the flip side. Her dad's landscaping business did well, but it required long hours and backbreaking work. At a young age, Susie decided it wasn't for her and announced: "I'm going to be a CEO!" She thought this direction would offer stability and be more rewarding. Susie's mom encouraged her to follow her ambitions, express her opinions, and never apologize for being herself.

With visions of conquering corporate America in her head, Susie worked in management positions for a number of different companies. She celebrated successes and received recognition along the way. But over time, the corporate world lost its shine. Toxic work environments took a toll on her mental health. Then, after that second layoff, it became clear to Susie she hadn't chosen the secure path at all. She decided it was time to create her own business. Not just any business—one that empowers others.

Susie envisioned a line of products to provide the kind of encouragement her mother gave her: Do what you want to do. Say what you want to say. Don't apologize for who you are. She'd always found cursing a powerful form of self-expression and an emotional release, so Susie began brainstorming ideas with a friend. Fingerless gloves had become a staple in cooler office climates, so they came up with a pair with a bird embroidered on each of the middle fingers. That's how Flip'em the Bird was born.

Today, in addition to gloves, the line includes winter hats and T-shirts. Susie also launched a giveback initiative called "Swearing Is Caring," which she uses to champion causes close to her heart, like supporting and destigmatizing mental health. For Susie, Flip'em the Bird isn't meant to be an aggressive "fuck you," but rather an irreverent and fun form of self-expression for anyone who's felt like they've needed to change who they are to fit in. She imagines a movement where everyone feels free to "flip them birds up!"

BE YOURSELF; EVERYONE ELSE IS ALREADY TAKEN.

OSCAR WILDE

PART 2:
THE SPICE

THE C-WORD

I entered the word "teratoma" into the WebMD search bar and scoured the results. A rare type of tumor with hair, teeth and bone. I'd heard about this kind of thing before. No, I'd seen it on an episode of "Grey's Anatomy." A man thought he was pregnant, and an emergency surgery revealed that what he thought was a baby was a teratoma. I surmised that my diagnosis was like those featured in many episodes of "Grey's"— freakish conditions that made for a dramatic storyline but didn't happen much in real life. What if I'd mistaken my teratoma for a pregnancy? What if I'd named and celebrated the candy bar-sized tumor on my right ovary as a new life that I would soon bring into the world with my cheating and now ex-boyfriend? I laughed out loud. I'd dodged a bullet. No baby. Just a growing glob of mixed matter tissue that I decided to call Penelope. Penny for short.

On the morning of my preoperative assessment I casually Googled the surgeon who'd be extracting Penny. I hadn't thought of it before that. He was, after all, one of the best gynecologic surgeons in the city, according to the staff at my OB-GYN's office. My search revealed a man in his 40s with dark wavy hair who'd graduated from Duke and was an associate professor at the University of Minnesota Medical School. That was all I needed to know. I dressed up for the appointment. A black-and-white print A-line dress, black tights, knee-high designer boots—the first pair I'd really splurged on, paying the equivalent of a half-month's rent.

I was in my 30s and in the best shape of my life, a size 6. The last time I'd been a size 6 was in second grade. Now I was a vegetarian who had lost a bunch of weight and walked 5 miles a day. I ate organic. I never smoked. I wasn't a big drinker. This surgery would be a breeze.

As I sat up, shifting my bare bottom awkwardly on the crinkling paper of the exam table, a threadbare medical blanket draped over my lap, the surgeon said something I never expected to hear. "I'd like to get you in for surgery to remove the tumor this Friday, and you'll start chemotherapy right after."

"Chemotherapy?" I asked, completely confused. The doctor who'd first discovered Penny had said that mature cystic teratomas were almost always benign. "How do you know it's cancer?"

"It's definitely cancer," he said, looking me directly in the eyes.

"But … I thought it was a teratoma?" I asked.

"No," he said.

"A harmless tumor with hair and teeth?" I insisted.

"It's not a tumor with hair and teeth; you have ovarian cancer," the doctor said, sounding slightly annoyed now, as if he'd never been questioned. His look was serious.

I'd just lost my own dad suddenly and unexpectedly to cancer a few weeks before. Ovarian cancer had taken my mom's life a decade earlier at age 57. No one had said anything about Penny being cancer. If I had thought there was a chance I had cancer, I would have had someone in the room with me—my best friend, my aunt, someone who could help me navigate something so monumental.

"I need to talk this over with my family. And I'm in the middle of a big website project at work," I explained to the doctor, hoping to delay the conversation.

"I don't think you understand," he said, his eyebrows knitting together. "This surgery needs to happen as soon as possible."

I had ovarian cancer surgery that same week. Removal of both ovaries and fallopian tubes, the peritoneum and a dozen or so lymph nodes in my groin. Chemotherapy started before my wounds had fully healed.

I'd officially left the radio industry six years earlier and launched a communications consultancy. I worked all over the country managing public relations for a traveling museum exhibition. Now, during the crux of my medical issues, I was working for a museum in Minneapolis. What I thought would be a short-term contract position had turned into a four-year fulltime gig. I never intended to be there that long. But the museum's mission to educate and innovate was close to my heart. I'd developed great friendships with many of my colleagues. And the building and grounds were lovely. There was just one problem: It was not the right fit for my personality.

The woman I reported to there had said on numerous occasions that she found it difficult to work with me. The first few years we worked together, she commended my positivity. More recently, she'd begun scolding me for laughing too often and too loudly. Initially she praised me for challenging the way things had always been done and taking a fresh approach. Now she said I was too assertive, and it was making others uncomfortable. With every criticism, I'd tamp down my personality to please her, but it never worked. I wondered if—and secretly hoped—my cancer diagnosis might change the way she felt about me.

It didn't. After my third round of chemotherapy, while I was still working fulltime, she called a meeting with HR. I was formally reprimanded for an incident earlier in the week, where I disagreed with a co-worker about how an event would be handled in my absence. She said there'd been an erosion in my relationships with staff over the past two months. I reminded her that I'd just lost my dad and was undergoing cancer treatment. The next day, my oncologist mandated an eight-week medical leave.

Just a couple of weeks after I returned to work, that same supervisor presented me with two options: accept a newly created lower-level position with a substantial cut in pay or a severance package. It had nothing to do with me, she said. It was about organizational effectiveness. Instead of accepting either, I quit.

I didn't have a fully developed plan for what I'd do next. And there was less than $1,000 in my savings account. But I felt free and fearless. I imagined nothing could be scarier than staring death in the face and telling it to get the hell out of my way. Nothing could be worse than wondering whether my body would survive having organs removed and getting pumped full of hazardous waste for four months. Next to cancer, whatever came next would be a walk in the park.

What I came to realize was that my gregarious nature and go-get-'em attitude worked well in the radio industry, where rambunctious was the norm and everything moved at breakneck speed. It suited me well when I was a consultant for the traveling exhibit because it operated like a circus where we'd spend a whirlwind six months in one market and then pull up stakes in a day and move on to the next city. A museum that was led by a team content to live in the past and comfortable with the status quo was not the right fit for my personality.

INSTRUCTION

PERSONALITY AND STRENGTHS

My dad's process for making spaghetti sauce was always the same. Once his giant stockpot was filled with colorful chunks of tomatoes and other veggies, it was time for the spice. That was when he'd begin adding his secret blend of seasonings. He never used any measuring tools; he simply added the seeds, powders and flakes by the handful.

Dad liked all of his food spicy, including his homemade sauce. He always said, "The spice is what makes the sauce your own." I finally learned what he meant when I was all grown up and tried to recreate his recipe on my own for the first time. I quickly realized that his blend was one that could not be replicated by anyone other than him—though I tried several times.

For the purpose of your Whyography, think of the spice as your special blend of mannerisms, quirks and personality traits—the things that make you stand out as an individual. The spice is your sense of humor, your demeanor, your attitude. It's how your customers get to know you before they actually know you or meet you in person. And you get to decide how much or little spice you'd like to add to your Whyography. You determine your secret spice blend.

A great way to get a better understanding of your personality type and how it has influenced your career path and the development of your business is to take a personality assessment. There are many personality tests out there, and you've probably taken some of them. Even if you have, I encourage you to do so again—think of it as a refresher. It's possible for personality traits to become more or less dominant over time, depending on what's happening in your life.

The assessment and exercises that follow will provide valuable insights about who you are and why you do things the way you do. They're key pieces of helping you further illustrate your WHY.

EXERCISE: PERSONALITY ASSESSMENT

Start this exercise by taking the 16Personalities online personality assessment. Go to www.16personalities.com.

Answer the assessment questions honestly. Remember, you are the only person who will see your answers. After you've completed the assessment, you'll see a summary of your personality type along with additional details about how you approach your life and work. This information will be used in the next exercise and will help you identify what is most relevant to your story.

After you've completed the 16Personalities online personality assessment, print or save PDFs of each category of your results. If you request the results via email, you will receive a summary only. You will refer to your results in each category in future exercises.

EXERCISE: PERSONALITY ASSESSMENT REVIEW

Next, review your personality assessment results from 16Personalities. As you reflect upon your personality type, aspect, role and strategy, write down your thoughts about the results for each category. Were there any surprises? Are there details that seem particularly relevant to your role as a business founder? Do you recognize any direct connections to the work you have chosen to do?

1. What is your personality type?

Adventurer	Advocate	Architect	Campaigner
Commander	Consul	Debater	Defender
Entertainer	Entrepreneur	Executive	Logician
Logistician	Mediator	Protagonist	Virtuoso

2. Do your personality type and the way the assessment describes you ring true? What are your initial thoughts about the results?

3. What is your personality aspect in the MIND category?
   Extroverted   Introverted

4. Do your personality aspect in the MIND category and the way the assessment describes you ring true? What are your initial thoughts about this result?

5. What is your personality aspect in the ENERGY category?
   Intuitive   Observant

6. Do your personality aspect in the ENERGY category and the way the assessment describes you ring true? What are your initial thoughts about this result?

7. What is your personality aspect in the NATURE category?
   Feeling   Thinking

8. Do your personality aspect in the NATURE category and the way the assessment describes you ring true? What are your initial thoughts about this result?

9. What is your personality aspect in the TACTICS category?
   Judging   Prospecting

10. Do your personality aspect in the TACTICS category and the way the assessment describes you ring true? What are your initial thoughts about this result?

11. What is your personality aspect in the IDENTITY category?
    Assertive   Turbulent

12. Do your personality aspect in the IDENTITY category and the way the assessment describes you ring true? What are your initial thoughts about this result?

13. What is your personality role?
    Analyst   Diplomat   Explorer   Sentinel

14. Do your personality role and the way the assessment describes you ring true? What are your initial thoughts about this result?

15. What is your personality strategy?
    Confident Individualism
    Constant Improvement
    People Mastery
    Social Engagement

16. Do your personality strategy and the way the assessment describes you ring true? What are your initial thoughts about this result?

EXERCISE: PERSONALITY TRAITS

This exercise explores your personality traits and the quirks that make you one of a kind and your story uniquely yours. It's often a challenge to describe your own personality traits objectively, so begin by asking an individual who holds you in the highest regard (and knows you well) to review the list and select all of the personality traits they would use to describe you. Next, review the list—including their selections—and select traits you'd use to describe yourself. Work quickly; go with your gut and don't spend too much time overanalyzing. List additional personality traits if necessary.

Adaptable	Chic	Eccentric
Adventurous	Classy	Eclectic
Affable	Clever	Elegant
Affectionate	Common	Emotional
Aggressive	Communicative	Empathetic
Agreeable	Compassionate	Encouraging
Ambitious	Complex	Energetic
Amiable	Confident	Enthusiastic
Amicable	Conscientious	Exclusive
Amusing	Considerate	Exotic
Anxious	Courageous	Exuberant
Argumentative	Courteous	Fair-minded
Arrogant	Creative	Faithful
Authentic	Cultured	Family-oriented
Boastful	Decisive	Fearless
Bold	Delicate	Fiery
Boring	Dependable	Flamboyant
Bossy	Determined	Flexible
Brave	Diligent	Forceful
Bright	Diplomatic	Frank
Broad-minded	Discreet	Free-spirited
Calm	Distant	Fresh
Careful	Distracted	Friendly
Casual	Driven	Frugal
Charismatic	Dry	Fun
Charming	Dynamic	Funny
Cheerful	Easygoing	Geeky

Generous
Gentle
Genuine
Good
Gregarious
Guarded
Happy
Hardworking
Hardy
Helpful
Honest
Hotheaded
Humble
Humorous
Imaginative
Impartial
Inclusive
Independent
Innovative
Insecure
Intellectual
Intelligent
Intentional
Intuitive
Inventive
Kind
Laid-back
Lighthearted
Loud
Loving
Loyal
Mature
Meek
Modern
Modest
Mysterious
Naive
Natural
Neat
Nice
Nurturing
Opinionated

Optimistic
Organized
Outgoing
Passionate
Patient
Patriotic
Persistent
Philosophical
Pioneering
Placid
Plucky
Poised
Polite
Powerful
Practical
Pretentious
Private
Proactive
Punctual
Purposeful
Pushy
Quick-witted
Quiet
Quirky
Rational
Refined
Regimented
Relaxed
Relentless
Reliable
Reserved
Resourceful
Romantic
Sassy
Scattered
Self-confident
Self-disciplined
Sensible
Sensitive
Serious
Shy
Simple

Sincere
Smart
Smart-ass
Snobby
Snotty
Sociable
Soft-spoken
Sophisticated
Sparkling
Spicy
Sporty
Straightforward
Strong
Studious
Stylish
Sweet
Sympathetic
Thoughtful
Tidy
Tough
Traditional
Trusting
Unassuming
Understanding
Unique
Versatile
Warm
Warmhearted
Welcoming
Wild
Willing
Witty
Wondrous

EXERCISE: PERSONALITY TRAITS (TOP 5)

Now that you've developed a list of personality traits, spend a few minutes looking through all of the traits selected by you and the person who knows you well and identify your top five. As you did with your values, narrow your list by eliminating any that you don't feel 100 percent connected to. Next, group similar personality traits together (e.g., warmhearted, thoughtful, considerate) and choose one trait that you feel best describes your personality in each group. Once you've narrowed it to five, list those traits and write a few sentences about how each of your unique characteristics has influenced your entrepreneurial journey.

EXAMPLE:

Self-disciplined. When I was growing up, whenever I decided I was going to try something new, I approached it with intention and care. I possess a natural ability to motivate myself and keep moving forward. This has served me well as an entrepreneur, as there is always something new to learn—I continually push myself to stay current.

EXERCISE: YOUR STRENGTHS

In addition to your personality, you bring a number of unique talents and gifts to the world. This exercise explores your strengths. Rather than self-assessing, you'll engage others, asking them to provide insights about your strengths.

Begin by making a list of 10 people who are not related to you whom you have worked with in a variety of capacities—perhaps you worked together as employees for another company. It could be someone you interacted with as the owner of your business, or as a volunteer, a member of a group, a mentor or mentee, etc. Contact the people on your list by email and ask them to describe your strengths.

One approach is to ask them to imagine you're among a group of people whose airplane made an emergency landing on an uninhabited island in the South Pacific. Use the example email below to learn their perceptions of your strengths. As you receive feedback from those you've reached out to, create a document with their responses.

EXAMPLE EMAIL:

I'm embarking on the process of writing my Whyography and currently working on identifying my unique talents, gifts and strengths. I've been challenged to imagine I'm among a group of people whose airplane made an emergency landing on an uninhabited island in the South Pacific. The plane is fully intact, and all of the crew and passengers are alive and well. None of the tracking or communications equipment is functioning. It's not clear when or if the plane will be located and everyone will return to civilization. Given our history together, would you be willing to imagine we're in this setting together and tell me one of the strengths you think I'd bring to this survival situation? And specifically, why you think I possess that strength? Thank you for providing your valuable insight.

WELL-BEHAVED WOMEN
RARELY MAKE HISTORY.

LAUREL THATCHER ULRICH

INSPIRATION

CARRIE BOE
SUPERSTRONGCHICK

Author's note: This is an edited version of the story Carrie Boe wrote while participating in a Whyography workshop.

The summer before Carrie Boe started fourth grade wasn't what she expected. Her mom had just been diagnosed with a debilitating illness. Then, as Carrie played in their backyard, running through the sprinkler, she slipped on the wet grass and broke her arm. Instead of carefree sunny days at the pool, she spent her time watching reruns of "I Dream of Jeannie" and eating bologna sandwiches. She couldn't bear the thought of losing anyone in her family. So she'd stand in front of the open fridge thinking about what to eat next, although she really wasn't hungry.

That pattern continued as her mom got sicker. When it came time to shop for new school clothes, Carrie found herself in the "Pretty Plus" section at Sears. When she was just 15, Carrie watched her mom slip away and her dad struggle with the loss by numbing himself with alcohol.

Carrie also numbed, but with pizza and fast food. In her 20s, Carrie was diagnosed with Type 2 diabetes.

By her early 40s, Carrie had lost her entire immediate family. She managed her grief by going to work, keeping social engagements and tackling her to-do list. And she kept eating. When she found herself weighing well over 350 pounds, Carrie had a powerful realization: She wasn't ready to die too. She resolved to get healthy, so she connected with a trainer named Kevin. He promised to be in it for the long haul if she was willing to commit. Though she could barely walk on a treadmill, Carrie bought a package of sessions. She also began working with a registered dietician on her nutrition.

Thanks to this crucial support, Carrie experienced a major shift. Instead of eating her way through life's challenges, she discovered how to be present and deal with the highs and lows. She learned to love herself and feed her body to fuel it rather than to numb it. She ended up losing the equivalent of an entire extra person and significantly increased her muscle mass. Insulin injections were no longer necessary. She also gave up her longtime corporate job and launched a wellness practice, SuperStrongChick.

As a certified health coach and personal trainer, Carrie helps her clients transform their lives through education, support and empathy. Through one-on-one and group coaching, workshops and community events, she connects with others who may relate to her experiences. Her mission is to empower women who are experiencing obesity-related issues to love themselves while achieving better health and wellness and discovering their best life.

Ultimately, Carrie demonstrates that health is not just defined by fitness and nutrition. Nor does losing a significant amount of weight automatically "fix" everything. Relationships, spirituality, careers and self-care all play a role in overall wellness. Embracing life's transitions and establishing good daily habits are the path to genuine happiness, renewed health, and true strength in mind, body and spirit.

JUNITA FLOWERS
JUNITA'S JAR

Junita Flowers had always dreamed of owning a business. She even started down the path to entrepreneurship not once but three times. Each time she was derailed by something she endured for more than a decade but kept hidden—domestic violence. But Junita's positive spirit prevailed. Somehow, she always found the strength to keep moving forward. She kept working toward her goal. She never gave up hope. The fourth time was going to be different.

Junita's respite from the dark moments in her life had always been baking. She found great pleasure in spending time in the kitchen—on her own and with her children. It was something she loved doing as a kid too, with her own mother and grandmother. As an adult, Junita began using the same recipes for cookies, cakes and desserts that had been handed down in her family for generations. It brought back memories of the stories shared around the kitchen table, and it grounded her in a joyful past.

Junita's original business vision was simple: share her all-natural scratch-made cookies with the world. She started with family and friends, delivering baskets filled with cookies during the holidays. As demand for her products increased, she decided to launch a website. Soon she was packaging and selling her cookies online.

The business continued to grow and so did Junita. She left the abusive relationship and went through a divorce. She began volunteering with organizations that served battered women and families. And as she transformed her own life, Junita realized her cookies could help transform the lives of others as well. In addition to providing for herself and her kids, Junita could use her business to be the change she wanted to see in the world. That's when she officially launched her social enterprise, Junita's Jar.

Junita is a strong believer that change happens through conversations—especially difficult ones. So she made a commitment to use Junita's Jar to facilitate meaningful discussions. Her "Cookies 'n Conversations" programming is designed to educate college students on relationship violence. The goal is to let them know that if they're experiencing abuse, it's not their fault, they're not alone, and there are resources available to help them. She hopes to create a community of support and inspire others to take action against domestic abuse. She donates a portion of the profits from her cookie sales to organizations that do the same.

There were times when Junita thought she might have been to blame for the abuse she received. She wondered if things would be different if she wasn't so outspoken. She knows now it had nothing to do with her. She has made it her personal mission to let others in abusive situations know that they too can break free from violence. And she has made it her business mission to "bake hope into every cookie purchase, helping women live their best lives."

MARY KAY ZINIEWICZ
BUS STOP MAMAS

Mary Kay Ziniewicz was certain she didn't want to be a mom. Her husband, Keith, didn't want kids either. And then the unexpected happened—they found out they were pregnant. When they saw their baby on the ultrasound for the first time, everything changed. Mary Kay and Keith fell in love with the tiny dot on the screen, and they couldn't wait to meet their daughter.

After Lily was born, the couple decided Keith would be a stay-at-home dad while Mary Kay worked in marketing and business development for two Twin Cities law firms. Then, when Lily turned 10, Keith went back to work and Mary Kay worked from home on the marketing consulting company she'd launched. As she waited with other moms at the bus stop, she began to notice one question the women asked each other regularly: "What are you doing today?"

Mary Kay realized how different her situation was from the other mothers. She had a successful business and a fulfilling career. Many of the moms were skilled professionals interested in working, but there were all kinds of barriers—family responsibilities, lack of support, scheduling constraints, guilt. She learned that more than 40 percent of women don't return to the workforce after their first child is born. Those who do face biases around availability, dependability, relevance and more. She began imagining a business model that would allow moms flexibility to work when, how and where it made the most sense for them and their families.

Mary Kay started to develop her concept in 2018 while continuing to work as a marketing consultant. This new venture pushed her outside of her comfort zone almost daily, and there were times she thought about giving up. That's when then-12-year-old Lily stepped in and built the company website, and Bus Stop Mamas officially launched.

With Lily as her chief technology officer, and the support of a team she calls her Super Mamas, Mary Kay developed a network of thousands of moms with various skills and backgrounds. They fill a critical need for hundreds of small to midsize businesses seeking workers in all kinds of positions—temporary, parttime, fulltime and more. Mary Kay calls it the #9to3movement, because she believes work needs to look different in the 21st century. The process for connecting moms and businesses is straightforward—businesses post any job opening that offers flexibility, and moms select opportunities that appeal to them. Mary Kay and her team make introductions, and the business owners and moms take it from there. The businesses pay a referral fee, while the women pay nothing to join the network.

Mary Kay now devotes 100 percent of her work time to what has become her second baby. She credits her first baby, Lily, and her husband for making the business possible. Though she may not have planned to be a mom, she now says it's the best thing that ever happened to her.

VAL FLEURANTIN TURNER
COACH VAL

Val Fleurantin Turner was living the life she had imagined for herself growing up in Haiti. She'd relocated from Florida to Minnesota for a software engineering job. She was a soon-to-be mom moving up the ranks at the largest medical device company in the world. She'd been invited to participate in an emerging leaders' program. But when the program required her to interview senior leaders within the company about their experiences, she noticed something concerning. They all expressed regret about not being there to raise their kids. Val immediately jumped off the leadership track.

Everything changed after that. Val was happy when she got to work on new projects, but it was short-lived. She accepted a new position at another large corporation, but she was still dissatisfied. She enrolled in an MBA program, which was challenging. Then she and her husband got divorced. Now she was juggling single parenthood, a demanding career and grad school. She was mentally and physically exhausted.

Without knowing what she'd do next, Val left her job and put her MBA on hold.

For a while, she felt stuck. She spent time working out because physical activity made her feel better. She immersed herself in her North Minneapolis neighborhood—something she hadn't done previously because she was too busy working. She discovered that while she lived in one of the healthiest states in the nation, her largely African American community didn't have access to the healthy food and health care it needed. On her way to pick up her son from day care one day, Val began praying in her car for a sign about what to do next. The answer that came: make an impact in the community through fitness. At the day care center, the director asked what she did for a living. When Val said she was in between jobs, the director replied, "You should be a fitness instructor." It was the confirmation Val needed. She decided to become "Coach Val," a certified Zumba instructor.

Val knew she could make the greatest impact by offering her fitness classes for free. But she'd gone from a six-figure income to no income, and her resources were dwindling. So rather than taking on the financial burden of her own studio space, she connected with community organizations in high-traffic locations. They agreed to let her use their spaces, and classes soon began filling up. As participants started sharing stories about how their lives were changing as a result of Val's programs, she wanted to do more. She became a certified lifestyle coach to expand her reach. Her goal is to create a healthy lifestyle movement that has generational impact in urban communities across the country.

Val couldn't be happier she jumped off the corporate ladder. It has enabled her to prioritize what matters most to her. It has also allowed her to follow in the footsteps of her grandmothers, who were successful business owners in Haiti, and whose example Val always knew she'd follow.

SUSAN ELWER
SPOONFUL APPAREL

Feeling embarrassed by a parent is a rite of passage for most teens. Susan Elwer felt something more like shame. Every week, as she and her mother walked up and down the grocery store aisles, she'd fixate on what was about to happen next. They'd get to the checkout, and when it was time to pay, Susan's mom would present the cashier with food stamps. Susan wanted to disappear. She just wanted to blend in with the rest of the families she saw paying with cash and happily leaving the store with big bags of groceries.

Growing up poor and relying on government assistance for food and medical care was hard on Susan's entire family. There were many times they had to go without things others took for granted. As a single parent, her mom did the best she could with what she had. Susan earned money babysitting to help out and focused on getting good grades in school. She was determined to go to college, get a good job and pull herself out of poverty.

Susan was always interested in helping others. She studied criminal justice in college. She interned for and eventually ran the supervised visitation program for a residential treatment center. After she got married, Susan shifted gears and worked in the corporate sector. Only she wasn't inspired by the work. After two children and a decade as a stay-at-home mom, Susan started thinking about her career again. She accepted a position at a public elementary school, assisting teachers and working directly with students who needed extra support. When Susan learned about a 4-year-old boy who'd gone without lunch the first three months of the school year, she made an extra brown-bag lunch every day until the school connected the boy's family with the services they needed. She hadn't forgotten what it was like to feel pangs of hunger deep in her belly, making it difficult to concentrate on studying or chores or just being a kid.

Susan felt something begin to rumble inside her again, but this time it was a desire to make a bigger impact—to feed more kids. Then one Sunday in church, the words from the sermon seemed to be aimed directly at her: "Don't judge, just love." She envisioned designing T-shirts with messages of love and acceptance and selling them to provide meals for hungry kids. She researched giveback businesses and realized she could have the most impact as a social enterprise donating a portion of the proceeds from merchandise sales to organizations already working to end hunger. She officially launched Spoonful Apparel in 2017.

Susan believes we are all here for a unique purpose, and through that purpose we make the world a better place. She says her purpose was placed in her heart that day in church. In three years, Spoonful Apparel has helped subsidize over 120,000 meals for kids in communities across the United States—proof of purpose in action.

PEOPLE WILL FORGET WHAT
YOU SAID, PEOPLE WILL
FORGET WHAT YOU DID, BUT
PEOPLE WILL NEVER FORGET
HOW YOU MADE THEM FEEL.

MAYA ANGELOU

PART 3:
THE SIMMER

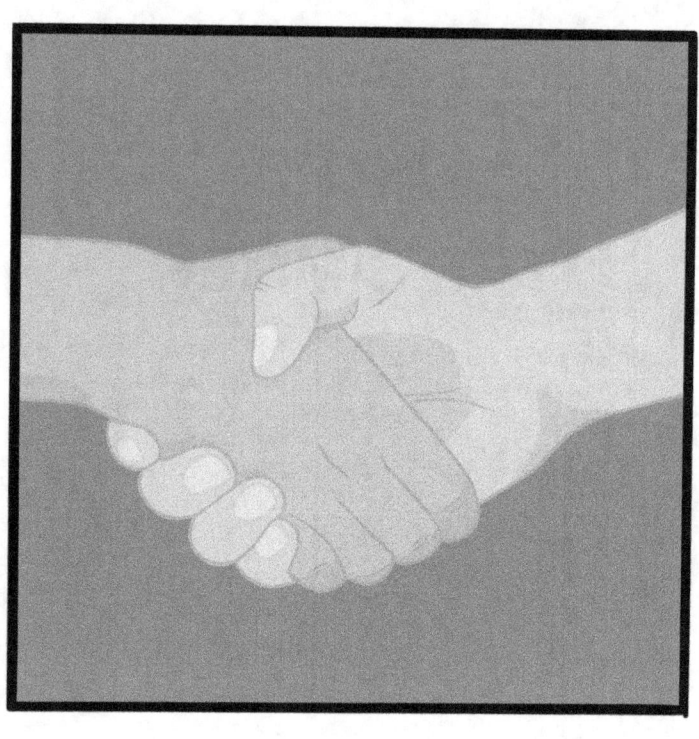

PEOPLE OVER PROFIT

I spotted him in the crowd at the Minnesota State Fair. And it was no small crowd. There was a record attendance that year. Over a million people had already passed through the turnstiles, and it was only halfway through its 12-day end-of-summer run.

I saw his eyes first in a sea of thousands of unfamiliar, sweaty faces. They were like large marbles the color of root beer, magnified to nearly twice their size by his glasses and illuminated in the August sun. He was my first real boss in radio, before the hip-hop station, at a rock station where I worked in my 20s—I'll call him Mike. There had been a revolving door of bosses before him, but they never lasted. He was my boss for five years or maybe more. This was the first time I'd seen him since I was laid off from that job two years earlier.

He was ambling along with his wife as if on a leisurely stroll in the park. They were talking and smiling, and they may have been holding hands, though I don't remember. Something began to wash over me. It felt like anxiety. Was it anxiety? What was I anxious about? Our eyes locked and he walked toward the live broadcast booth of the hip-hop radio station where I was currently working. There was a dance contest going on, and the DJ was giving away T-shirts. I was taking photos to post on the website.

"Chris!" Mike said enthusiastically, his hand outstretched. As he took my hand, he cupped it in both of his, lingering for a few seconds. "It's so great to see you!"

His eyes were kind. Warm. Sincere. The eyes of a teacher and mentor. A father-like figure. He had a little less hair than the last time

I'd seen him, and it was a little grayer around the temples. He looked well put together, as usual. Even his state fair wardrobe was business casual—a golf shirt and neatly pressed shorts. I thought about the last time we'd spoken. He called me at home the day after I was laid off. He apologized profusely, saying he knew nothing about it. He'd been traveling at the time, and the market manager had done the deed. He said if he'd known, it never would have happened. All I could think at the time was, "Then undo it."

It couldn't be undone. As the general manager of two radio stations in the Twin Cities, he was in his own precarious position. He'd been in a real-life game of chess with the general manager of three other stations in the market, which were owned by the same conglomerate. After an acquisition that brought all five radio stations under one umbrella, there was talk around town about one of them being ousted.

During that phone conversation, I told Mike he was the best boss I'd ever had. I meant it. My mom had been diagnosed with ovarian cancer two years earlier. He'd been supportive about me missing work to take her to chemo and various medical appointments. When she was actively dying and had two months to live, I told him I was moving into her house to be her fulltime caretaker. I requested the balance of my vacation time, which I planned to use to take Thursdays and Fridays off for the next eight weeks. A hospice nurse would fill in the gaps in the schedule when I wasn't there.

"You're not using your vacation time," he said quickly. "You take as much time as you need."

It was 1999 and working remotely wasn't a thing then, but he arranged for me to have a laptop with a connection to the company server so I could work from home—but only if I wanted to. When my mom died a couple of days after Thanksgiving, he called to ask if there was anything he could do.

"You've already done it," I said. "Taking care of my dying mother has been the greatest gift of my life."

"You were her greatest gift," he told me, his voice cracking.

His voice cracked again on the phone the day after I'd been laid off.

It was just two months after my mom's memorial service. He promised to do whatever he could to help me find my next job. I had a strong urge to tell him I loved him and that I was thankful he appreciated my outgoing and gregarious personality, believed in me, valued me, and taught me what it meant to be a compassionate leader who put people over profit. Instead I said we would talk again soon.

As it turned out, "soon" was two years later at the Minnesota State Fair. Since I'd last seen him, he'd quietly shifted into the market manager position. I was among dozens if not hundreds of people in the industry who thought he hadn't been treated well and that the higher-ups chose the wrong man for the head honcho position. There were rumors that he was going to retire, but that hadn't happened yet. Was I nervous because I didn't know what to say about how he'd been treated? He had spent his entire career contributing so much to the broadcast industry, and he was finishing out his days in a position that required nothing of him. He was filling his calendar with business breakfasts and lunches.

With all the hustle and bustle of the fair, I didn't get to say much. I came close when he asked how I liked working for my current boss.

"He's no Mike," I said.

"Well, that's probably for the best," he said with a big, hearty laugh.

We said goodbye, and he and his wife shuffled off toward the Sweet Martha's chocolate chip cookie booth. I got back to work. But I couldn't stop thinking about how much of an influence he'd had on my career and life. He set the bar high. Having someone believe in me at the start of my career changed my entire trajectory.

A MENTOR IS SOMEONE WHO ALLOWS YOU TO SEE THE HOPE INSIDE YOURSELF.

OPRAH WINFREY

INSTRUCTION

INFLUENTIAL PEOPLE AND EVENTS

The part of my dad's sauce-making process that fascinated me most came after all the ingredients had been stirred together in the pot and the flame on the stove was adjusted just right. "This is when the magic happens," he'd say. It didn't involve waving a wand over the pot to make dinner magically appear on the table. He meant it was time for the simmer.

Dad would let the sauce simmer on the stove for days, and my curiosity always got the best of me. I wondered how all those chunky vegetables managed to transform themselves into my favorite supper. I often got caught dragging a chair over to the stove to see what was going on in that great big pot. My dad would boost me up so I could take a peek.

I'd see thick red paste gurgling and rumbling like lava, rising up slowly and then sluggishly sinking back down into the pot. Sometimes a single bubble would make its way to the surface with a tiny explosion and a burst of steam wafting into the air. And then dozens more bubbles dancing and popping, breaking free with a spatter of red flying into the air and onto the stove, against the wall—some even parachuting their way down to the floor.

The simmer was a messy process and a crucial part of sauce-making. So much would be revealed. Sometimes the sauce needed more of something or the heat would need to be adjusted. My mom, my siblings and I would take a taste from the wooden spoon and give input. More salt. More garlic. More time. As my dad sampled his creation and made adjustments, he'd share stories about my grandma, her recipes, and how she taught him to cook.

Like sauce simmering on the stove, entrepreneurship is messy. Launching a successful business doesn't happen overnight, and we don't do it alone. These exercises are designed to get you thinking about the people and experiences throughout your lifetime that have played a role in the direction of your career and the creation of your business.

Some instruction as you work through the exercises: You are writing for yourself, so don't hold back. This part of the process may require more self-reflection than the previous exercises. Keep an open mind as you continue on this path to self-discovery.

You may need multiple work sessions for this section. In your initial session, start by reading through all of the questions. Write down the answers for those that come to mind right away and revisit the others later. Oftentimes, memories come up when you least expect it. The key is reading through all of the questions first. Your mind will continue to search for and reveal the answers in due time.

EXERCISE: YOUR INFLUENCES (A PRIMER)

This writing exercise is designed to get you thinking about the people and experiences that have influenced your career path and entrepreneurial journey. You may not have specific answers for every question right away, and that is OK. Take additional time to reflect and revisit the questions you don't immediately have answers for another time. It is important that you complete as much of this exercise as possible.

1. What were your favorite subjects/extracurricular activities when you were in school (grades K-12)? What made them interesting/exciting to you?
2. What books/literature did you read as a child/young adult that influenced your life? How did they impact you?
3. What music/art/media did you experience as a child/young adult that influenced your life? How did they impact you?
4. What films/television did you view as a child/young adult that influenced your life? How did they impact you?
5. What community service did you do as a child/young adult? How did it impact you?
6. When you were a child, what career/business/lifestyle did you imagine for yourself? Why did it interest you?
7. When you were a young adult, what career/business/lifestyle did you imagine for yourself? Why did it interest you?
8. When did you discover you were entrepreneurial and how did you come to the realization? What action did you take?

EXERCISE: YOUR INFLUENCES (AS A CHILD/YOUNG ADULT)

This writing exercise is designed to help you zero in on specific people and events—both positive and negative—that influenced the direction of your life and career. If you're unable to recall a person or event in one of the categories, give yourself time to digest the question and come back to it later. Start by thinking about your childhood up to age 18.

1. Family: Write about an impactful/influential family moment or event you experienced as a child or young adult. Who was/were the influential person(s) involved? What was your age at the time? Why does it stand out? What was/were the outcome(s) or lesson(s) learned?

2. Education: Write about an impactful/influential educational/school moment or event you experienced as a child or young adult. Who was/were the influential person(s) involved? What was your age at the time? Why does it stand out? What was/were the outcome(s) or lesson(s) learned?

3. Mentor: Write about an impactful/influential moment or event with a mentor/teacher/coach that you experienced as a child or young adult. Who was/were the influential person(s) involved? What was your age at the time? Why does it stand out? What was/were the outcome(s) or lesson(s) learned?

4. Career: Write about an impactful job/career moment or event you experienced as a child or young adult. Who was/were the influential person(s) involved? What was your age at the time? Why does it stand out? What was/were the outcome(s) or lesson(s) learned?

5. Major life event: Write about an impactful life event you experienced as a child or young adult (illness, death of a loved on, parents' divorce, moving, changing schools, etc.). What was the event? Who was/were the influential person(s) involved? What was your age at the time? Why does it stand out? What did you learn?

EXERCISE: YOUR INFLUENCES (AS AN ADULT)

Now think about specific influences on your career path as an adult and write about those specific people and events. Again, consider both positive and negative experiences you've had. If you can't think of a specific person or event in one of the categories, take some time away from the exercise and come back to it later.

1. Family: Write about an impactful/influential family moment or event you experienced as an adult. Who was/were the influential person(s) involved? What was your age at the time? Why does it stand out? What was/were the outcome(s) or lesson(s) learned?

2. Education: Write about an impactful/influential educational/college/ university moment or event you experienced as an adult. Who was/ were the influential person(s) involved? What was your age at the time? Why does it stand out? What was/were the outcome(s) or lesson(s) learned?

3. Mentor: Write about an impactful/influential moment or event with a mentor/teacher/coach that you experienced as an adult. Who was/ were the influential person(s) involved? What was your age at the time? Why does it stand out? What was/were the outcome(s) or lesson(s) learned?

4. Career: Write about an impactful job/career moment or event you experienced as an adult. Who was/were the influential person(s) involved? What was your age at the time? Why does it stand out? What was/were the outcome(s) or lesson(s) learned?

5. Major life event: Write an impactful life event you experienced as an adult (illness, death of a loved one, parents' divorce, moving, changing schools, etc.). What was the event? Who was/were the influential person(s) involved? What was your age at the time? Why does it stand out? What did you learn?

EXERCISE: WHYOGRAPHY JOURNEY MAP

A Whyography is typically a chronological account of your entrepreneurial journey. A Whyography Journey Map is a useful tool for tracking key events and people and determining their significance in your story. Mapping out milestones will help you continue to excavate memories and put them into context.

In this exercise, create a Whyography Journey Map by listing influential moments and major life events you identified in previous

EXAMPLE:

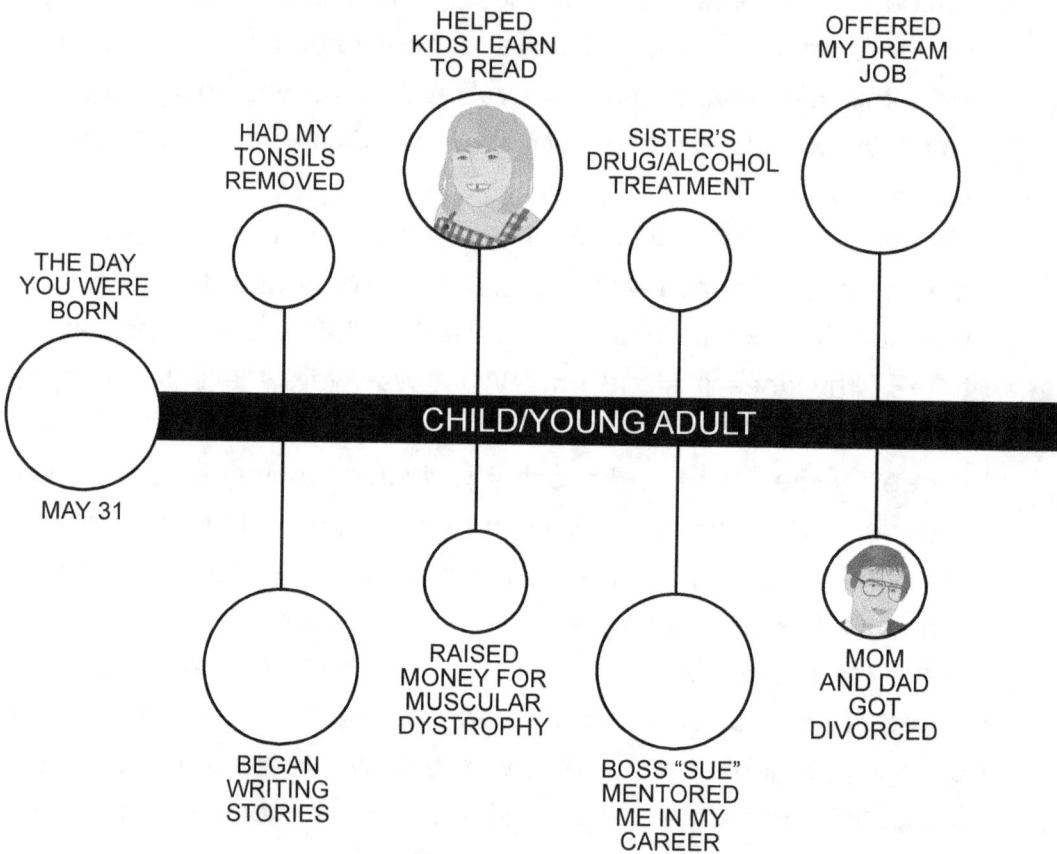

exercises on a timeline. Keep in mind, you may not include everything you capture on your journey map in your Whyography, but you'll appreciate having a record of it in the future (should you choose to write a memoir, for example).

Create your Whyography Journey Map using the example as your guide. Mark up your map, make a mess of it, and continue to add and refer back to it as you develop your story.

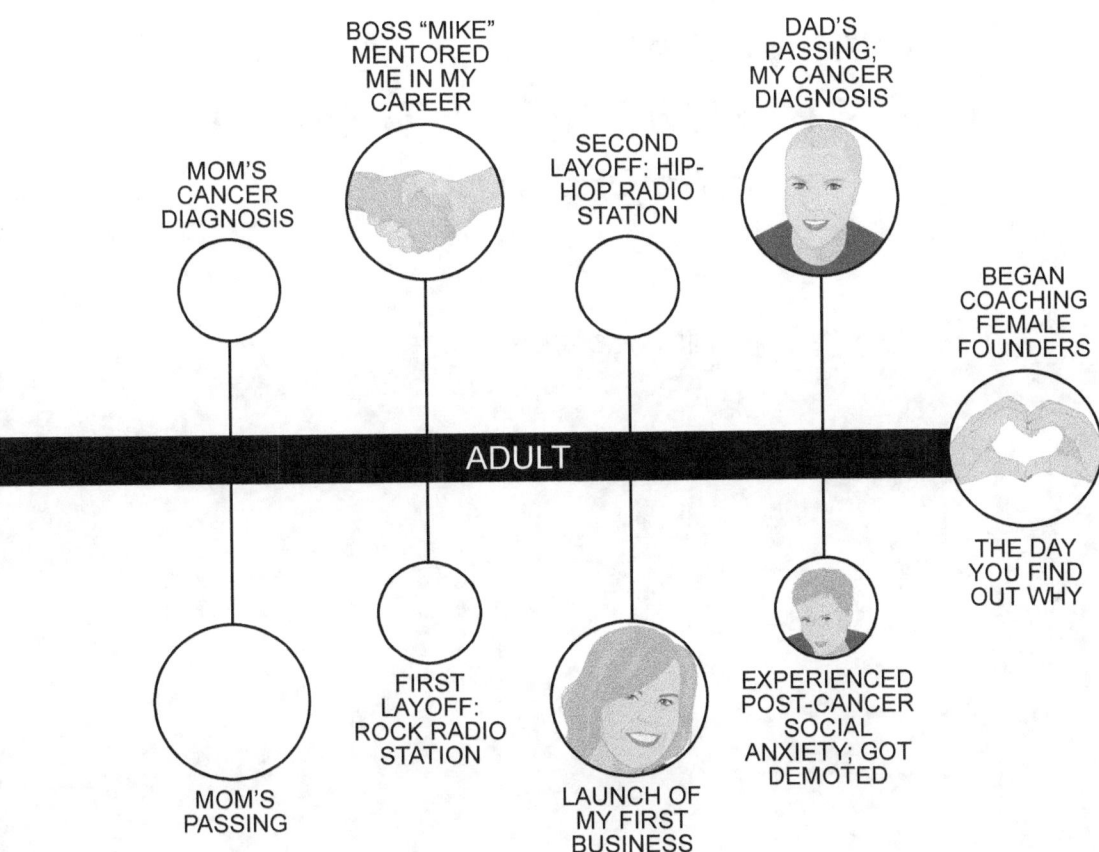

ANYTHING IS POSSIBLE WHEN YOU
HAVE THE RIGHT PEOPLE THERE TO
SUPPORT YOU.

MISTY COPELAND

INSPIRATION

LAUREN VANSCOY
ESSENCE ONE

Lauren VanScoy was sitting on the kitchen floor of a friend's house having an emotional breakdown. She wanted to be anywhere other than where she was in that moment. She hadn't seen her close girlfriends much since having her second baby several months earlier. But on that "girls' night in," her friends noticed something different about Lauren and were concerned. So they started asking questions. Where had she been? Why was she so distant? Was there something she wasn't telling them? Lauren didn't have any answers. She could barely speak at all.

She knew about postpartum depression but hadn't experienced it after the birth of her first child or even the first few months after her second baby. Now things weren't quite right, but she couldn't put her finger on it. She was struggling with social anxiety. Friends' social media posts were making her feel excluded and even paranoid. She couldn't figure out why it upset her so much, especially since she didn't want to leave the house anyway.

And then there was that moment on her friend's kitchen floor when it all came to a head. While it was incredibly painful at the time, it pushed Lauren to meet with a counselor. As it turned out, there was a medical explanation for what she'd been experiencing—major depressive disorder manifesting as anxiety. She learned about treatment options and worked with her doctor to get her medication right, and her mood improved significantly.

Lauren also discovered aromatherapy and essential oils, which immediately helped relieve her anxiety. Finding a balance of Western traditional medicine and all-natural remedies was life-changing. It inspired her to become a certified aromatherapist. She formulated her own products at home and officially launched Essence One in 2016 while she continued to work fulltime. She sold her products online and participated in special events on evenings and weekends.

At those events, Lauren educated hundreds of women on the benefits of living a life free of the toxins often found in beauty and home products. She also shared the role natural remedies played in transforming her own health. As she talked about her anxiety and depression, she heard from countless others who'd experienced similar issues. She realized how important it was to talk about mental health to help eliminate the stigma associated with it. She began donating a portion of her business proceeds to organizations dedicated to mental health education.

In 2018, Lauren took the leap to fulltime entrepreneurship. As she connected with other women-owned businesses, she discovered many shared her philosophy about giving back to the community. She proposed a partnership to five other women—Ginger Neilon of Baubles and Bobbies, Anna Hagen and Nikki Hollerich of Hagen and Oats, Robyn Frank of Thumbs Cookies, and Sairey Gernes of Urban Undercover. Their joint retail venture, Six for Good, launched in 2019. All six women are committed to putting people and the planet over profit. Each donates a portion of sales to causes she is personally committed to.

GINGER NEILON
BAUBLES AND BOBBIES

Ginger Neilon's mom was rushed to the emergency room. It led to a shocking cancer diagnosis, a major surgery and an emotional hospital stay. "If anything happens, I'll raise the girls," Ginger promised. She was in her 20s and adored her two youngest sisters—ages 8 and 10 at the time. She treated them like they were her own daughters. She invited them for sleepovers at her house and chaperoned their school field trips. Ginger knew that kind of reassurance was what her mom needed. And she meant it.

Ginger had been working in health care and decided to go back to school to become a registered nurse. But after taking a required elective course in art, Ginger realized being a nurse wasn't what she was interested in. She'd always been artistic, and now she considered putting her creativity to work as an interior designer. There was just one problem: The university had discontinued its interior design program.

Ginger arranged an internship with a local interior designer and boutique owner. She thought it'd help her decide if interior design was the right path. While Ginger learned the ins and outs of the business, the owner discovered Ginger made jewelry in her spare time. She asked her to create some original items to sell in the store. Customers couldn't get enough of Ginger's designs. As demand increased, Ginger finally realized what she was truly meant to do. She officially launched Baubles and Bobbies in 2014. Her jewelry collections are inspired by nature, and each piece is designed to make a statement.

Though Ginger's mom beat cancer, she experienced ongoing health issues. After an extended stay in the hospital and returning home to begin hospice care, she asked Ginger if she and her husband would follow through on adopting the girls. Ginger had inherited many wonderful traits from her mom, including a deep devotion and commitment to family. She assured her mom she would make good on her promise to adopt her sisters.

After losing their mother, and in a new role as mom herself, Ginger began to see the world through a different lens. When she learned how common sex trafficking is—particularly for vulnerable young girls in rural areas—she wanted to make sure her sisters were safe. As her business grew, Ginger realized she could use it to support causes that were important to her. She chose to start donating a portion of her proceeds to organizations working to stop sexual exploitation of girls and women.

In early 2019, Ginger became part of a joint retail venture called Six for Good with five other female founders—Lauren VanScoy of EssenceOne, Anna Hagen and Nikki Hollerich of Hagen and Oats, Robyn Frank of Thumbs Cookies, and Sairey Gernes of Towel Topper and Urban Undercover. It was a perfect fit and the right time for Ginger to expand her business. She feels fortunate to be collaborating with others who are as passionate about giving back as she is.

NIKKI HOLLERICH AND ANNA HAGEN
HAGEN AND OATS

Anna Hagen spied a giant industrial band saw collecting dust in her in-laws' garage and became obsessed. It hadn't been touched for some time, but she had an idea for an art piece she wanted to make for her fireplace mantel—if she could just get her hands on that saw. Anna mentioned it to her husband, who talked his parents into letting them take the saw. As the couple drove home with the huge piece of machinery wedged into their vehicle, Anna called her sister, Nikki Hollerich, to tell her the news. Nikki shared her enthusiasm for the newly acquired power tool, and they set a date to work on the project together.

In their free time, the sisters often did crafts together. When they were kids, they spent time with their dad in the garage, fixing cars and building a wood strip canoe. That's when he'd share life lessons. He'd encourage them to not be limited by gender biases and to pursue their passions, regardless of what others might think.

After a bit of research and some practice using their new tool,

Anna and Nikki got to work, sketching and cutting out the silhouette of a buck on a large piece of lumber. There was more cutting. And then distressing, sanding and staining the wood. The result was a one-of-a-kind art piece perfect for above the fireplace. When they posted a photo of their handiwork on social media, the reactions were overwhelmingly positive. People wanted to place orders. So the sisters began making more pieces to sell. Each time a buyer displayed one online, they'd get more requests.

Both women had careers they loved—Anna as a marriage and family therapist and Nikki as director of operations for a national restaurant franchise. While they never officially planned on launching a business, they were having a blast doing it as a side hustle. In 2016, they found a brick-and-mortar space in Newport, Minnesota, and officially launched Hagen and Oats, a business specializing in custom wood décor, signage and game boards.

Today, they have a team of mostly female employees. The sisters take great pride in challenging biases about which industries and jobs women should work in and about what women are capable of—like operating power tools and doing carpentry. Empowering women is foundational to their business, and they love seeing its impact. "It's amazing to see how a woman's attitude and posture completely changes after she uses a nail gun or power saw," Anna said.

Hagen and Oats is also committed to giving back. Its "Stainbow" collection of rainbow stained art initially benefited victims of the mass shooting at a gay nightclub in Orlando and today supports a number of organizations that serve the LGBTQ+ community. Anna and Nikki are also part of Six for Good, a retail venture developed in partnership with four other Minnesota women business owners dedicated to using their purpose-driven businesses to make a difference in the lives of others and the world.

ROBYN FRANK
THUMBS COOKIES

When she wasn't waiting tables or auditioning for acting roles, Robyn Frank often wandered around New York City ducking into neighborhood bakeries. A transplant in a city known for its culinary diversity and delights, Robyn had yet to find one specific treat that reminded her of her Minnesota roots. Surely there was a New York baker who'd created something similar to her mom's tiny, buttery, melt-in-your-mouth "thumb cookies." Named for the gentle thumb press she'd give each quarter-sized mound of dough before baking them, they were the very definition of comfort. But Robyn couldn't find anything like them anywhere.

Robyn's acting career hadn't exactly gone as planned, and her gut was telling her to do something different. So she started making her favorite tiny cookies in her apartment kitchen and hit the pavement again. This time, instead of bakeries, she popped into local small businesses to share samples and ask buyers if they were interested in selling her cookies. Eventually, a handful of stores bought—that's when she officially launched Thumbs Cookies. Robyn's big break came while she was waiting tables at the Ace Hotel in Midtown Manhattan. The hotel's general manager asked Robyn what she did when she wasn't serving. When she told him, he asked, "Why don't we sell your cookies here?" A few days later, they were hashing out details for Thumbs Cookies to be included in the hotel's VIP amenities basket.

Thumbs Cookies continued to gain traction over the next two years as Robyn's side hustle. She wanted to transform her life from waiting tables to becoming a fulltime businesswoman. Eventually, she realized she'd be able to get traction more quickly if she moved back home to Minnesota. She relocated Thumbs Cookies to the Twin Cities, where she could afford commercial kitchen space and focus on scaling the company. Robyn's friends and family back home immediately rallied around her, just like she knew they would. They spread the word with their networks about her products. They showed up at the farmers market and pop-up events where Robyn set up shop. It ended up being one of the best decisions she's ever made.

As demand for her products grew, Robyn invested in an apparatus she calls "Kranky," which pushes out perfectly portioned disks of dough. More important to Robyn is the dedicated team she's invested in. She works side by side with her cookie-making crew and prides herself in creating a collaborative and joyful culture where everyone loves coming to work. She believes in putting people first.

She is also committed to giving back. Thumbs Cookies is a member of Six for Good, a retail collaborative in Minnesota. The six female founders in the group are dedicated to using their purpose-driven businesses to make a difference in the lives of others and the world. A portion of Thumbs Cookies' sales are donated to Students Demand Action, a national initiative dedicated to ensuring school and community safety.

SAIREY GERNES
URBAN UNDERCOVER

Sairey Gernes rearranged the contents of her suitcase over and over again, trying to make everything fit. She sat on top of it and tugged at the zipper, but it wouldn't budge. There wasn't enough room for all the gear she wanted to bring along on her trip. She knew what had to go: the bulky towel wrap. Of course, the resort would have towels. But Sairey was bunking up with a large group of women on this trip. She really wanted her towel wrap, with its built-in elastic band. With it she could walk around freely without the possibility of exposing herself to her travel companions. In that moment, Sairey felt a product idea coming on.

The only difference between her towel wrap and a regular towel was the elastic that held the wrap in place. That led Sairey to create a simple solution to a common problem—the Towel Topper. It's an elastic band designed to be used with a standard bath towel. It keeps your towel in place and your hands free. Plus, it takes almost no room in a suitcase.

And it's not just for travelers. It's perfect for the gym, beach, dorm or home.

The Towel Topper wasn't the first product Sairey developed based on need. Sairey launched her first business, Urban Undercover, in 2009. As a women's size 12 or 14, she couldn't find underwear that was made well, fit well, and was also pretty. Her friends laughed when she announced her business idea, reminding Sairey that she didn't wear underwear. That was the point. She'd given up trying to find something foundational to every wardrobe because what she needed didn't exist. So she decided to introduce a line of beautiful everyday underclothes designed with traveling in mind. The underwear can be rolled into a pocket in the back of the waistband—perfect for tucking into a purse, overnight bag or suitcase.

Her product line expanded to include more fashionable yet functional travel-inspired apparel and accessories—from multipurpose leggings that hold their shape during all kinds of adventures to comfy signature wraps that function as both a sweater and a blanket. As a purpose-driven brand inspired by her own travels around the globe, Sairey believes Urban Undercover has a responsibility to develop, design and make all of its products ethically. That means using smarter sustainable fabrics and demanding high standards in manufacturing.

Sairey believes traveling connects us—to each other, to the earth, to our history—and makes us better people. She also believes people are better together. She's teamed up with other women business owners who share a commitment to leading with purpose through a Minnesota-based retail collaborative, Six for Good. The boutique has two locations in the Twin Cities and features products exclusively from female founders dedicated to using their businesses to make a difference in the lives of others and the world. All of the businesses donate a portion of their profits to causes close to their hearts.

**HOW WONDERFUL IT IS THAT
NOBODY NEED WAIT A SINGLE
MOMENT BEFORE STARTING TO
IMPROVE THE WORLD.**

ANNE FRANK

PART 4:
THE SECRET
INGREDIENT

WHAT FUELS YOUR PURPOSE

I was 5 years old and helping to set the table for dinner when there was a knock at the front door. From the kitchen my mom shouted for me to go see who it was. I ran to the window that looked out onto the porch. To my surprise, it was my kindergarten teacher with a large wrapped box.

"It's Mrs. Kay!" I shouted back. "And she brought a present!"

I don't recall a word of the exchange between my mom and my favorite teacher as they stood in the entryway. I couldn't take my eyes off the box. After what felt like a lifetime, my mother handed it over. I tore into it and was awestruck. It contained dozens of perfectly sized compartments that held small servings of my favorite snack foods—cans of nuts, packets of crackers, wedges of cheese, cylinders of salami. I'd never seen anything like it.

By the time I started kindergarten I was an enthusiastic reader and writer of stories. It wasn't until I was among my peers in the classroom that I realized some kids my age had not yet learned to read or write. I had a difficult time wrapping my 5-year-old brain around this. It broke my heart that one of my friends, a boy named Troy, was ushered out of the room because he stumbled on his words while trying to read aloud. Had he done something wrong? Was he being punished? Could I help him learn to read the way my big sister had helped me?

After talking with my mom about it, she began volunteering at my school. Together we—but mostly she—tutored kids who needed help learning to read. Mrs. Kay was thankful for the support. She dropped off the treats to show her appreciation.

That was the first time I recall seeing something I didn't like in my very small world and wanting to change it. It happened again the summer I turned 7. This time, I was inspired by a TV commercial for a national nonprofit. The spokesperson encouraged viewers to raise money for new treatments for muscular dystrophy. One of the ways to help was to host a backyard carnival. I wanted more than anything to help sick people get better. And with the offer of a free carnival kit, I was all in.

The kit arrived by mail. It included tips for creating the event, game tickets and a pledge form. I decided on games and emptied my piggy bank to buy prizes from the corner store gumball machine. I created a puppet theater from a giant cardboard box and puppets from brown paper lunch bags. I made gallons of cherry Kool-Aid. I recruited friends and family to help staff the event. I went from house to house spreading the word.

When all was said and done, my event generated around $20 in coins. I exchanged the cash for a check from my mom, which I proudly mailed to the nonprofit. I received a certificate recognizing my efforts. I learned many valuable lessons from my first official fundraising event. The greatest lesson of all: I could make a difference in the world.

The desire to do good and give back got stronger as I got older. It wasn't until I began working with a Minnesota-based economic development agency dedicated to helping women and minorities start and grow small businesses that I discovered my WHY. My work included partnering with startup entrepreneurs on marketing initiatives. I also taught the marketing curriculum for a brand-new intensive business-planning course. During the last session of the multipart course, participants were required to pitch their business to a panel of mock investors.

I'd been looking forward to pitch day for weeks. I was certain the graduates from the inaugural class would kick ass pitching their businesses. They knew their stuff. These women were super smart, self-assured and well spoken. They courageously brought great ideas to life and were passionate about what they created. But as we gathered in the classroom and prepared for pitch fest, there wasn't the joyful buzz of excitement I expected. Instead, there was a dull drone of dread.

"Isn't this exciting?" I cheerfully asked a cluster of women, hoping to divert any negative thoughts they might be having.

"I'm nervous," one of the women said. "It's like we're on 'Shark Tank.'"

"No one's going to eat you alive here; it's more like a guppy bowl," I said with a chuckle.

The women were not amused.

As I watched each of them take their place at the front of the room to make their pitch, nothing seemed to go as planned. They struggled to operate the computer and the projector. They struggled to look at the panel and the audience directly. They struggled to speak at a volume that could be heard in the back of the room. They struggled to confidently communicate their business purpose and impact. They didn't seem at all prepared.

It was painful to watch. I had been cheering these women on for months. I wanted them all to crush it. Instead came the crushing realization that the program may have failed them. I may have failed them. The odds were already stacked against female-identifying founders—women in the U.S. receive significantly less support and business funding than their male counterparts. Women of color receive even fewer resources than white women. A business plan would do them no good if they couldn't effectively pitch their business.

Watching those fledgling entrepreneurs flounder on pitch day was a lightbulb moment for me. There was something I could do to ensure female founders didn't struggle when it came time to pitch their business. I could give them the tools and support they needed to confidently communicate their WHY and share their story with the world. And I could use my business to deliver this mission.

FIGHT FOR THE THINGS YOU CARE ABOUT, BUT DO IT IN A WAY THAT WILL LEAD OTHERS TO JOIN YOU.

RUTH BADER GINSBURG

INSTRUCTION

CLARIFY YOUR WHY

Some experts say finding your purpose is as straightforward as finding what breaks your heart. It's true, your WHY could be influenced by heartbreak—your own or someone else's. But if you're a compassionate person driven to change the world—and perhaps have been since you were a kid—you could likely name several things that break your heart. And purpose isn't just connected to heartbreak, grief, anguish or distress. It's influenced by all kinds of emotions and many different experiences, both positive and negative.

You've done the meaningful work of identifying influential moments throughout your entrepreneurial journey and listed them on your Whyography Journey Map. It's highly likely the moments you listed were accompanied by intense emotions, and that's why you considered them influential. As you clarify your WHY, rather than focusing on emotions (like what breaks your heart), focus on what came next. In other words, what came after you experienced something you considered an influential moment in your life? What action did you take? And more specifically, how did your values guide your actions?

Keep in mind that action doesn't always immediately follow the actual moment something influential happened. Sometimes it takes weeks or months or even years before you recognize the significance of the event or are ready to do something. You may have experienced a setback, and something similar may have happened again and again before you took action. You may have forgotten something caused you pain until you witnessed someone else going through it, and their pain and memories of your own experience inspired you to do something about it.

For example, as a taller-than-average Black teenager attending a school where the majority of students didn't look like her, Shawntan Howell often felt like she didn't belong. There were times throughout her life and career when she felt like an outsider and her confidence wavered. When her daughter had a similar experience, the heartbreak Shawntan felt as a teen came rushing back. It's what inspired her to launch Girls Are Powerful, an organization dedicated to lifting up and empowering girls.

When Susan Elwer was growing up, her single mom struggled to put food on the table, and Susan often went without. Susan dreaded trips to the grocery store and wanted to disappear when her mom would pay with food stamps. As an adult working at an elementary school, when Susan learned about a student going without food, memories of her painful childhood reemerged. It led her to launch Spoonful Apparel, a social enterprise supporting organizations that feed the hungry.

The key to clarifying your WHY is making the connection between the influential moments in your life and the values that guided the outcome and ultimately pushed you toward business ownership.

EXERCISE: YOUR WHY DETECTOR

This exercise is designed to help you clarify your WHY, pinpoint your purpose, discover your North Star, identify your secret ingredient. Create your WHY Detector using the example as your guide.

EXAMPLE:

INFLUENTIAL MOMENT	ACTION	OUTCOME	VALUES
Seeing a friend get exiled from the classroom as he struggled to read aloud	Advocated for kids who needed help reading	Helped create a volunteer program to support kids' literacy	• Equality • Inclusion • Fairness • Education • Empowerment
Learning about kids confined to wheelchairs who are too sick to run or play	Planned a fundraising event to support kids with a debilitating disease	Raised money for medical research	• Empathy • Kindness • Generosity • Community • Inclusion
Being demoted at my job following cancer treatment	Launched a fulltime communications consultancy	Built a community of empowered women business owners	• Health • Independence • Integrity • Community • Empowerment
Watching fledgling female business founders flounder and fail when pitching their businesses	Coached women on communicating their business purpose and impact	Developed a program that has supported hundreds of women	• Empowerment • Equality • Education • Inclusion • Diversity

Fill in the "INFLUENTIAL MOMENT" column first, listing relevant influential moments and major life events you listed on your Whyography Journey Map. Then, working row by row, fill in the remaining columns.

Start by focusing on the influential moment and reflecting on what came next. What action did you take following that moment? Write it in the "ACTION" column. For example, as a kindergartner, after seeing my friend Troy exiled from the classroom as he struggled to read aloud, I advocated for kids who needed help reading by asking my mom what we could do to help. While my action was immediate, that's not always the case. The action that follows an influential moment can happen months or even years later.

Next, in the "OUTCOME" column, list the result of you taking action. The outcome of my advocating for kids who needed help reading was the development of a volunteer-led tutoring program at my school. Again, my outcome was immediate, but it could also come later. Don't get hung up on the timing.

Now, think about the values that guided you when you took action and helped drive the outcome. List five in the "VALUES" column. If need be, refer to your values list and your Values in Action Tracker. On your tracker, you made connections between the brands you listed and your personal values. Here, your goal is to make connections between the influential moments and the values that helped you navigate those moments and what came next.

Once your WHY Detector is completely filled in, look for recurring themes. What are the values that continue to show up as you navigate life and career? For me, empowerment, education and equality are enduring values that emerge in both my personal and professional life. These values are connected to the difference I want to make in the lives of others and inform my WHY.

EXERCISE: YOUR TINY WHY STATEMENT AND WHY STATEMENT

During live Whyography workshops, this is the point in the process when, inevitably, at least one participant will say, "If I tell you about my business, will you tell me my WHY?" And I get it. You may know you're fueled by purpose. You may care about getting clear on your WHY. You may have a desire to share it with the world in your brand story and brand. It sure would be great if someone could save you some time, wave a magic wand and simply tell you your WHY.

Spoiler alert: There is no magic wand. But a Tiny WHY Statement (TWS) is the next best thing. It's typically five to seven words. And developing your TWS is simply combining your business name with a power verb (PV) and your ideal customer (IC).

Your PV is a powerful descriptor that communicates action. It's a single word that is directly connected to your WHY and says a whole lot about you and your business. It helps to illustrate the impact you're making (or hope to make) in the lives of others—specifically, your IC—and it provides insight about the values and strengths you bring to your business.

EXAMPLES:

Advances	Elevates	Mentors
Advocates (for)	Empowers	Nurtures
Assists	Enables	Prepares
Boosts	Encourages	Promotes
Champions	Guides	Serves
Develops	Helps	Supports
Educates	Invests (in)	

Your IC is a specific person or group that benefits most from the products and/or services your business offers. The person whose problem you are truly solving. It is important to narrow down your audience. Resist the urge to cast a wide net and go with something like "people" or "individuals." Instead, be as specific as you can.

EXAMPLES:

Female-identifying business owners
Professional women
Busy moms
Underrepresented children
Organic farmers

To create your TWS, use this template (business name + your PV + your IC):

1. (Business name) _____
2. (your PV) _____
3. (your IC) _____

EXAMPLES:

- Publish Her empowers female-identifying business owners and authors.
- (Business name) mentors professional women.
- (Business name) supports busy moms.
- (Business name) invests in underrepresented children.
- (Business name) promotes organic farmers.

To make it more powerful, transform your TWS into a WHY Statement by tacking the words "so that they" onto the end of it and adding an impact statement. Create as many versions of your WHY Statement as you like, but keep it as short as possible—it should be easy to remember and recite.

To create your WHY Statement, use this template:

1. (Your TWS) _____
2. SO THAT THEY (your IMPACT/result of bringing your WHY to the world) _____

EXAMPLES:

- Publish Her empowers female-identifying business owners and authors so that they achieve entrepreneurial success.
- (Business name) mentors professional women so that they receive the advancement opportunities they deserve.
- (Business name) supports busy moms so that they can focus their time on what matters most.
- (Business name) invests in underrepresented children so that they have an opportunity to thrive.
- (Business name) promotes organic farmers so that they can serve more families.

When you've created a few versions that feel right to you, ask yourself these questions to be sure your TWS and WHY Statement clearly articulate your WHY:

- Does this statement reflect my personal values?
- Does this statement illustrate the personal strengths I bring to the table?
- Does this statement articulate a problem my business solves?
- Does this statement speak to something bigger than me?

EXERCISE: YOUR PITCH ON PURPOSE

Earlier I shared my experience watching the women who'd participated in a business-planning course as they struggled to make their pitch to a mock panel of investors. Soon after, I began working one-on-one with women entrepreneurs, coaching them on communicating their business purpose and impact. Through that process, the Pitch on Purpose template was born.

In this exercise, build on your TWS and WHY Statement to develop your Pitch on Purpose. Think of your Pitch on Purpose as your elevator speech. It's a bit longer than your TWS and WHY Statement, but it's still intended to be a brief statement. It's what you'd say if you only had a minute to describe your business and its connection to your purpose. As you continue writing, imagine you're giving this pitch to someone on an elevator and you have their attention for less than a minute. Keep it concise.

To create your pitch, use this template:

1. MY NAME IS _____
2. I'M THE FOUNDER OF _____
3. A BUSINESS DEDICATED TO (your PV + your IC) _____
4. BY PROVIDING/OFFERING (your WHAT/your products and/or services) _____
5. TO SUPPORT THEM IN (problem your products and/or services solve) _____
6. SO THAT THEY (your IMPACT/result of bringing your WHY to the world) _____

EXAMPLE:

My name is Chris Olsen. I'm the founder of Publish Her, a social enterprise dedicated to empowering female-identifying business owners and authors by providing tools, resources and community to support them in clarifying and communicating their purpose, so that they achieve entrepreneurial success.

PEOPLE DON'T BUY WHAT YOU DO, THEY BUY WHY YOU DO IT.

SIMON SINEK

INSPIRATION

MELISSA TAYLOR
BEAUTY LOUNGE

When Melissa Taylor was a little girl, she dreaded getting her hair done. She never liked how it turned out. She observed other girls who loved their hair, and she noticed a direct connection between how they felt about their hair and their self-esteem. As a teen, she started styling other people's hair as a way to express her creative side. What she enjoyed most was seeing the boost of confidence people would get. But Melissa never imagined being a hairstylist or owning a salon one day.

After attending a career fair in college, Melissa narrowed her options to two companies. One of them was Target Corporation in Minnesota, which recruited her for its leadership development program in the financial services area. Melissa decided to jump into corporate life and relocated from Atlanta to Minneapolis. After three years, she longed for something more. That's when she started doing hair for weddings on weekends.

Melissa quickly realized she was making more money working two days a week as a hairstylist than she was in two weeks at her day job. And she was having a lot more fun. So she rented a chair on a trial basis, doing hair at a bridal salon. She loved it so much she ended up leaving Target. And when the woman who owned the salon announced she was selling it, Melissa took a leap of faith and took over the lease. In 2011, the salon now known as Beauty Lounge Minneapolis was born.

Owning a salon was harder than Melissa anticipated. Some stylists left when the original owner left and Melissa upped chair rental slightly. That meant she needed to spend time networking and finding new stylists. She knew getting the right people was key to building the business. As a Black woman, it was important to Melissa that everyone felt like they belonged there. She wanted the stylists to be skilled in working with all hair types—she'd seen untrained stylists fail too often when working with African American hair textures.

As she found the right people and found her groove, Beauty Lounge began to make a name for itself. She became known for her commitment to changing the beauty industry. And after discovering YouTube channels featuring untrained individuals instructing parents of biracial children on how to do their hair, Melissa launched the Texture Academy and started offering classes taught by professionals.

Today, Melissa describes her salon this way: "We're not a Black salon, we're not a white hair salon, we're not a curly hair salon, we're not a natural hair salon. We're a salon for people who value diversity. We are challenging the norms in our industry, hoping to create a shift." Melissa is on a mission to show girls with dark skin and textured hair they are beautiful exactly as they are, and they don't have to change the way they look to measure up to anyone else's standards of beauty.

LAURA KELLER
PIXIE DUST

Laura Keller was on top of the world. She was living in Los Angeles and about to start a job at a prestigious advertising agency. She was ready to hit the ground running. But before she'd even set foot in the agency's door, she got a call from her would-be boss. He informed her the Los Angeles office was closing. "The good news is you'll receive one year's salary," he announced. "The bad news is you no longer have a job."

The news caught Laura completely off guard. But she didn't wallow in it. She'd also been planning her wedding and had discovered a hole in the market for modern yet classic, tasteful and unique wedding décor and accessories. So Laura found a solution: She began sourcing items from designers and vendors who were not specific to the wedding industry. She developed wedding category exclusivity agreements with those designers, launched Divine Weddings in 1998 at the start of the dot-com boom, and sold the products on a first-of-its-kind website.

Laura's vision for a successful business quickly came to fruition, and the competition was taking notice. In fact, one of the biggest players in the wedding industry began copying her product designs. She met with them and proposed they buy Divine Weddings. They weren't interested—they'd already copied her business model. Squashed by a much larger competitor, Laura closed her business in 2001. She didn't see it as a failure. It opened her eyes to the world of entrepreneurship, and she knew she'd start another business eventually.

When Laura's then-husband's job required that they move to Minneapolis, Minnesota, she took a contract position for an advertising agency there, tapping into her numerous industry contacts to recruit creative talent. When the senior recruiter left the firm, Laura stepped into the role and began working with outside consultants. Once again, she recognized a hole in the market. No one was recruiting in a strategic way.

In 2007, Laura and business partner Ashley Mehbod—also an agency veteran—launched Pixie Dust, an executive search firm specializing in supporting creative agencies and marketers looking for leaders who can champion new ways of thinking. And more specifically, Pixie Dust is focused on female leadership. Women are grossly underrepresented in chief marketing officer and senior-level creative positions, and Pixie Dust is on a mission to do something about it. As the name implies, the agency provides clients with the magic ingredient to enhance, elevate and improve their business—the people. Along with their talent scout, Lisa Hashbarger, they work to continually build and expand their network of the best creative problem solvers in the industry.

Laura's focus on women's equality extends beyond her work at Pixie Dust. In 2017, she met social entrepreneur and humanitarian Wendy Diamond, the founder of Women's Entrepreneurship Day (WED). WED is an international event that empowers women and girls to become active participants in the economy. WED engages program ambassadors all over the world to fulfill its mission, and Laura serves in that role for Minnesota.

LEANNE ARANADOR
LADORU

Leanne Aranador had endured the harshest insults. Like salt in a wound, they were hurled at her during the times when she was feeling her most vulnerable.

"It's because you have no value," after a co-worker refused to acknowledge Leanne's contribution to a project.

"You know you're not worthy, right?" when a job interview Leanne thought might turn into something didn't pan out.

"It's no surprise he didn't call back," when a connection with a potential match didn't go beyond a first date.

The words were unkind and untrue. But they held a lot of power over Leanne. And they weren't coming from someone else—they were lies she'd been telling herself for a long time.

It wasn't until the artist and illustrator made a New Year's resolution to doodle every day for an entire year that she began to see the truth. It was an experiment suggested by a friend—intentional daily doodles. As she doodled, Leanne began to realize there was a different voice inside her. It wasn't harsh or demeaning. For the first 208 days of doodling, it was a faint whisper. On day 209, a major transformation occurred. The voice was louder than the one that'd been telling her lies for so long. And through the art she was creating, Leanne realized that imperfections were actually points of interest. Doodling had unleashed her true and powerful voice, and through it she could turn vulnerabilities into strengths.

Leanne made a promise to herself to honor that voice every day moving forward. She began combining her doodles with advertisements she thought were bland, transforming them into works of art. She expanded her repertoire of surreal illustrations, using them to tell compelling stories in her freelance design work.

Doodling also sparked an idea for a purpose-driven business. Leanne envisioned an art-infused clothing brand as a means to encourage other women to wear their voices and transform their lives and the world around them. In 2018 she launched Ladoru, a collection of apparel and accessories featuring combinations of her doodles with messages of purpose, transformation and vulnerability. For Leanne, the greater meaning behind Ladoru is a desire to transform one's pain, circumstance or situation into something beautiful and purposeful that will inspire others.

While entrepreneurship is not for the faint of heart, and it's often a test of courage and confidence, Leanne's transformation has empowered her to overcome fear and self-doubt. She finds strength in sharing her voice with the world and in the connections she's made with others while pursuing her purpose. She is most grateful for the people she's been able to bring together throughout this journey—those who share similar values and who, like Leanne, believe "our words shape our world."

Leanne wants to bring inspiration to both closets and minds. "Just like you choose your clothes every day, you can choose the words and thoughts you put on." She hopes she is inspiring women to choose to wear compassion, kindness, humility, strength and love.

SARAH MOE
SLEEP HEALTH SPECIALISTS

Sarah Moe was on a path to the career she imagined for herself when something unexpected happened. "You're in the wrong room," her college professor told her. There weren't many people of color at the small-town Wisconsin university where Sarah was studying elementary education, and all eyes were on her as the instructor asked to see her schedule. When Sarah provided proof she belonged in the course, the professor still wasn't satisfied. She asked to see Sarah's student ID. Sarah fought back tears as she handed it over. Finally, the professor relented and told her to sit down.

The instructor didn't acknowledge she'd humiliated Sarah or even apologize. Sarah's head swirled as she tried to understand. She thought about the hockey jersey she wore to class—was it too casual? Others were dressed casually, and their presence wasn't questioned. She'd been singled out because the professor thought she didn't look like she belonged. Not only did the exchange make Sarah uncomfortable, but she felt truly unwelcome.

As a result, Sarah left the university and returned to Minnesota. She began to rethink her plan to become an elementary school educator and considered her interest in health sciences instead. As she explored options, Sarah learned about the field of sleep study. She took a course and was hooked from the get-go. She went on to pursue an education in sleep study and got licensed in polysomnography. Sarah had found her new career path.

For several years, Sarah worked overnights conducting sleep studies in a clinical setting. Her dad had worked the overnight shift at a local newspaper when Sarah was growing up, and she'd always been a night owl herself. She loved working one-on-one with patients, educating them about sleep health and seeing the dramatic shift in their quality of life. Some burst into tears of joy when they awoke in the morning after using a continuous positive airway pressure (CPAP) machine for the first time.

Outside of the clinic, Sarah was getting lots of questions about sleep. She often wondered why, since one-third of a human's life is spent asleep, sleep health wasn't taught in school the same way exercise was. She'd been teaching courses at a local college but wanted to reach a broader audience, so she created a business model for a new venture.

Sarah launched Sleep Health Specialists in 2015. Her aha moment came when she realized she could partner with businesses to educate their workforce about sleep health. Sarah now shares her expertise through customized lunch-and-learns, classes and seminars. She also conducts sleep assessments and provides action plans to improve team members' sleep quality. Ultimately, Sarah shows companies how well-rested employees are healthier and more productive, which benefits the organization's bottom line.

Today, Sarah couldn't be happier with her career path and believes it was diverted away from elementary education for a reason. She has found her true calling.

KERI BISCHOFF
KERI BISCHOFF CONSULTING

Author's note: This is an edited version of the story Keri Bischoff wrote while participating in a Whyography workshop.

Keri Bischoff felt like she'd just been punched in the gut. "You'll never earn what you do here—especially for a woman your age," her boss said as she announced her resignation. It was a low blow and left her momentarily breathless. She quickly realized his words were a gift. They confirmed what Keri already knew. She'd made the right decision. She was ready to take a leap of faith and start her own business.

Years earlier, Keri had discovered a tool called Clifton StrengthsFinder. When she learned her results, she was blown away. Finally, she had answers about where she naturally excelled and why she approached things the way she did. She sat her whole family down and shared the details. She explained her top strength was "Learner," meaning she loved to ask a lot of questions, discover new things and go to school.

It provided clarity to her family and helped Keri articulate feelings she hadn't been able to explain.

A few years later, when a friend asked Keri to attend a certification course in Omaha for StrengthsFinder coaches, she had no plans to leave her current job. But she'd been a proponent of the tool since discovering its impact on her own life and witnessing its transformative results for others. So Keri headed to Omaha with her friend, open to new possibilities and not fully knowing where it would lead.

Completing the course was transformational for Keri. Suddenly she knew it was time to leave her job, and she set a goal to launch her business on the first day of 2015. And though her boss didn't take the news well, Keri began building her coaching practice and creating her own workshops. She came alive when she presented with her "Woo" and "Communication" strengths. Her "Learner" and "Input" strengths helped her learn from expert leaders and create collaborative work teams. The process of building a business challenged her, but she never gave up— it satisfied the "Achiever" in her.

Today, Keri works with a wide range of individuals, from nuns to neurologists, to help them clarify their unique strengths. By showing them their potential—and blind spots that could be holding them back— she empowers them to become better leaders, team members, and business owners, as well as to build stronger organizations. They're able to show up as their true, authentic selves. Keri believes the world will be a powerful place when we're all understood and valued for who we are and the strengths we bring to the world.

Keri is also passionate about supporting emerging female leaders to understand their value. So she created "Stillwater Alumnae Program: Girl Power." Through it, girls at her high school alma mater learn from successful female graduates who hold nontraditional roles. Keri's mantra when it comes to people of all ages embracing their strengths: "If you can see it, you can be it."

I WRITE ONLY BECAUSE THERE
IS A VOICE WITHIN ME THAT
WILL NOT BE STILL.

SYLVIA PLATH

PART 5:
THE SAUCE

PAINT BY WORDS

It was a freezing cold morning in January. In spite of the subzero temperatures, the sun was a blazing ball of white light in the cornflower blue sky. As I sat at my desk working, a murder of crows squawked verbosely outside. The frequency and volume of their caw-cawing distracted me. I got up from my chair, wrapped my thick wool cardigan sweater around me tightly and looked out of my office window.

I peered up at the 100-year-old white pine tree in front of my house. My eyes scanned the stubs of the bald limbs that had cracked off near the top of the tree long ago and then darted to the branches of the other naked trees nearby. I couldn't spot the crows' shadowy figures anywhere. They were close, though, and so loud I wondered if they were angry or distressed about something. Or maybe they were just celebrating, I thought. Perhaps they were thankful for the sunshine and rejoicing in spring's imminent arrival.

As I sat back down, I thought of my mom. It had been nearly 20 years since she'd passed, and I still thought of her every time I heard a crow call out. She reminded me of a crow. Her hair was black and wavy and shiny. Her eyes deep and intense. She loved nature, my part Native American mom—spending time in nature, learning about nature, honoring nature.

Growing up, my family took camping trips near the Boundary Waters Canoe Area in northern Minnesota—close to the Canadian border— nearly every summer. My favorite part was hiking in the woods with my mom. Hiking was simpler back then. No one cared about high-performance shoes for navigating the rocky terrain or synthetic fabrics meant to wick away moisture. It was more of a "hike as you are" kind of thing. We wore the same T-shirts, shorts, sneakers and flip-flops we wore all summer. My mom had a pair of Dr. Scholl's sandals with clunky wooden soles like clogs. They made a clopping noise as she walked through the woods, and as I trailed behind her I often imagined we were on horseback.

She called our hikes adventures. We'd follow a well-worn trail looking for birds and bugs and berries. We'd eat wild raspberries and blueberries right from the bush. I'd fill a bucket with as many as I could find, and she'd promise to use my bounty to make campfire coffee cake for breakfast—a mixture of Bisquick, milk, eggs, sugar and berries, poured into a pie tin and baked on an open flame.

"Listen to the cicadas singing!" she'd say, calling my attention to the high-pitched screechy mating call of the male insects. She explained they were the only bugs capable of producing such a unique and loud sound, and that it was meant to attract a mate while simultaneously stopping birds from eating them. It also meant they were dying.

She'd veer off the path and find a scenic spot to set up her easel and canvas. She'd prop up her small wooden suitcase filled with foil tubes of paint and horsehair brushes. Then she'd sit and paint beautiful pictures of the forest as I looked for gnome houses in the trunks of the trees or lay on my back daydreaming and staring up at the canopy of pine trees. She taught me that crows were the wisest of all birds. She said some Native tribes even believed crows could talk. I would strain to hear the crows, hopeful I could make out what exactly they were saying.

Right after she died, I noticed whenever I left the house a crow would call out from the treetops. "Hi, Mom!" I would holler back.

As these memories flooded my mind on that January morning, I realized in an instant: That day was her birthday. She would have been 76. I wished more than anything we could've been celebrating together. She adored celebrations almost as much as she treasured the woods. She loved hosting, cooking and giving gifts. She took great pride in decorating the house, planning the menu, and selecting and wrapping the presents. My heart began to swell as I realized how much I missed her.

And then suddenly I heard scratching and fluttering outside my office window. I turned my head slowly and froze as I saw a beautiful black bird peering in at me.

"Hi, Mom," I said, my eyes stinging with tears.

I gently reached for my phone to take a photo.

"Please don't go," I said quietly, desperate to capture the moment in an image outside of my brain.

She didn't go. I took her picture, she stayed for a minute longer, and then she flew away.

IF THERE IS A BOOK YOU WANT TO READ, BUT IT HASN'T BEEN WRITTEN YET, THEN YOU MUST WRITE IT.

TONI MORRISON

INSTRUCTION

WRITE YOUR STORY

When I was in my 20s, I tried to talk my dad into mass-producing and selling his homemade spaghetti sauce. I even designed a label for the jar thinking I could convince him. His sauce was better than any brand available at the grocery store, and everyone who'd tasted it agreed. His response was always, "No way! My sauce is only for people I like!" He'd also remind me how much work it was to make a batch—as if I hadn't watched him make it all those years.

After following his proven process for making each pot of sauce, and with all the time, effort, and love he invested, the end product—that savory, garlicky, spicy sauce—was definitely worth it. Think of your Whyography as your one-of-a-kind special recipe—the result of your time, effort and love. But unlike my dad, who was only willing to share his sauce with a select few, get ready to share your story with the world.

In this section, you'll learn a proven storytelling structure and begin writing your Whyography. First, a reminder about the differences between a Whyography and a basic business bio. Your LinkedIn profile is an example of a basic business bio. It includes all the basics, like your education and the jobs you've held. It's loaded with facts, but it lacks heart. It's all stats and no story. It certainly doesn't showcase who you truly are. It's focused on your WHAT and not your WHY.

Leading with your WHY is important for female business founders. Women continue to face significant hurdles in launching and growing small businesses, like limited access to funding and resources. The ability to confidently communicate your purpose and impact can help put you at an advantage. Funders are more likely to invest in you.

Consumers are more likely to support and recommend you. Employees are more likely to stay and succeed with you. Leading with your WHY sets you up for business success from the get-go.

A Whyography combines the power of purpose and the principles of storytelling to honor your journey and what it took to get where you are today. It communicates your values and the difference you're making in the world. A Whyography, and the process of developing it, gives you the confidence to share your story with the world and lead with your WHY.

LESSON: ARTICULATING YOUR WHY

Before you begin writing, you'll need to decide which point of view you'll use. Whyographies are typically written from a third-person point of view, with the narrator referring to the characters by name or with the third-person pronouns "he," "she" and "they." Other points of view in writing are second person, in which the storyteller uses the pronoun "you" to address the audience, and first person, which features a character in the story serving as the narrator and using the pronoun "I."

Depending on where you intend to publish your story (e.g., your company website, marketing materials, etc.), it will likely need to be narrated by someone other than you. It may feel awkward writing about yourself in this way initially, but you'll get used to it. There are benefits to narrating your story in the third person—it can help free up inhibitions you may have about talking about yourself. It also lets you put yourself in your audience's shoes and get a better idea of how they'll interpret the information. If you intend to write a longer version of your Whyography (e.g., a memoir or business book), you'll want to write it in the first person.

In this lesson, you'll learn about the art of storytelling and a story arc called Freytag's Pyramid, which you'll use as the framework for your Whyography.

German writer Gustav Freytag developed Freytag's Pyramid in the 1800s. Through extensive research, he discovered that stories that were a big hit with audiences all had something in common. Each followed a specific formula that included—in this order—an exposition, a rising action, a climax, a falling action and denouement. Shakespeare actually mastered this proven dramatic structure in his five-act plays, and the formula is still used in bestselling books, movies and theater today.

1. EXPOSITION

The exposition is the setup of the story. It provides background information about the main character, the story setting and any basic conflict. The exposition includes an inciting moment, which sets the rest of the story into motion. In a Whyography, the inciting moment could be one of the influential events you listed on your Whyography Journey Map. It could involve the loss of a job, a relationship, someone close to you, a home or something you cherish. It might be a birth, a significant milestone, or a big discovery about yourself or a family member. It could be a historical event or something you considered "a sign" that you were meant to pursue a certain path or go in a specific direction.

2. RISING ACTION

Next, the rising action is the series of events and actions that move the story toward the climax. During rising action, the basic conflict introduced during the exposition can be complicated by secondary conflicts. As the main character, that means you may have encountered obstacles and challenges that prevented you from reaching your goal. In a Whyography, this is often the point where an entrepreneur identified a problem or issue and developed products and/or services that could solve the problem, resolve the issue, or make a difference.

3. CLIMAX

The climax is the peak of the action and the turning point in the story. As an entrepreneur, this could be the moment you realized you had to pursue business ownership. Everything changes after the climax. Things that may not have gone well start looking up. If the story is a tragedy, the opposite occurs after the climax; things that were going well begin to go wrong. In a Whyography, the climax often begins right before you decided to take the leap and pursue entrepreneurship.

4. FALLING ACTION

The falling action is when the story reverses, the conflict begins to unravel and the main character wins (or loses). The falling action sometimes contains a moment of suspense, which causes the final outcome to be in doubt. In a Whyography, the falling action is typically an overview of the business purpose and provides detail about how you're making a difference in the world. Ask yourself: What purpose does your business serve? What's your mission? What's your WHY, and how and why are you bringing it to the world?

5. DENOUEMENT

The denouement—French for conclusion—is where the story ends and the main character is better off than she was at the beginning. Or, if it's a tragedy, it ends with sadness or loss. In a Whyography, the conclusion is often a summary of the impact the business has had to date. It could also include your vision for the future.

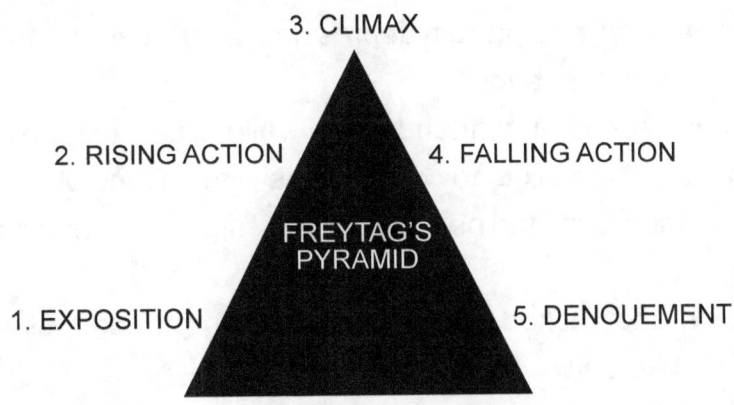

EXERCISE: WHYOGRAPHY FRAMEWORK

The goal of this exercise is to build the framework for your story. You'll want to have your Whyography Journey Map on hand for quick reference. Start by creating a document listing the five sections of Freytag's Pyramid ("EXPOSITION," "RISING ACTION," "CLIMAX," "FALLING ACTION" and "DENOUEMENT"). Under each section, write a few lines about the key moments captured on your journey map. For now, write the information in bullet points—you'll transform it into sentences and fill in more detail later.

Lauren VanScoy is the founder of two Minnesota-based companies, Essence One and Six for Good. Her story is featured in this book and is used as an example throughout this section.

1. EXPOSITION

EXAMPLE:

- Lauren had a second baby, was anxious about leaving the house
- She knew about postpartum depression, hadn't experienced anything like it after her first baby
- She hadn't seen her girlfriends for a while, was experiencing FOMO, but had no desire to go anywhere or be with anyone other than family
- Lauren's friends invited her over for girls' night, she reluctantly agreed to join
- That night they asked her what was going on, expressed concern, Lauren broke down
- Lauren had a mental breakdown on the kitchen floor with her friends, couldn't explain what she was feeling

2. RISING ACTION

EXAMPLE:

- The breakdown pushed Lauren to make an appointment with a counselor
- She was diagnosed with major depressive disorder, her depression was manifesting as anxiety
- She was given medical treatment options, wanted to research all options available
- Lauren learned about aromatherapy and essential oils
- She experienced immediate relief and less anxiety with aromatherapy

3. CLIMAX

EXAMPLE:

- Lauren experimented, found the right balance of traditional medicine and natural remedies, it was life-changing
- She was eager to learn more about natural remedies and decided to become a certified aromatherapist
- She began making her own aromatherapy and natural cleaning products at home
- Friends and family tested her products and loved them, encouraged her to sell them
- Lauren decided to offer her products to the masses and officially launched Essence One as a side business while she continued working full time

4. FALLING ACTION

EXAMPLE:

- Lauren launched a website, manufactured all of her own products, sold them online
- Began participating in marketplace events and pop-ups, met other amazing female business owners
- Loved hearing their stories and felt empowered sharing hers, learned that countless others had experienced depression and anxiety
- She realized her WHY is to support individuals struggling with mental illness, so that they know they're not alone and there are resources available
- Lauren realized she could use her business to do more than create amazing products, began donating a portion of her proceeds to organizations dedicated to mental health education

5. DENOUEMENT

EXAMPLE:

- As the business grew and Lauren connected with more female business founders, she recognized the power of collaboration
- She proposed the idea of a new venture and partnership to five other women
- Together they launched Six for Good—a shared retail space featuring brands from purpose-driven companies committed to putting people over profit
- Six for Good began offering retail space to emerging entrepreneurs in the store so they can showcase their products
- Now Lauren and team are considering expanding the Six for Good concept to other markets

ADDITIONAL CONSIDERATIONS

Before you move on, review your bullet points and be sure you've included the following:

- Does your exposition include a tense or dramatic moment?
- Does your rising action include a problem you discovered and a high-level overview of the products and/or services you developed to solve it?
- Does your climax include details about your business launch and more information about your products and/or services)?
- Does your fall action include a summary of your purpose or your WHY Statement?
- Does your denouement include details about your impact and vision for the future?

LESSON: THE BRAIN ON STORIES

Next, you will transform your bullet points into your first draft of your Whyography. But first, it helps to understand the science of storytelling and the effect stories have on the human brain. A quick disclaimer: I'm not a neuroscientist. You probably aren't either. The good news is you don't have to be one to understand the brain on stories. I've boiled down research from experts, and in this lesson I share key points to help you tell better stories.

Neurons are minuscule messengers in the brain and spine. They use electrical and chemical signals to communicate and control various bodily functions. When you tell a story to someone, the neurons in the listener's brain begin to imitate the neurons in yours. It's called neural coupling, and it's why scientists believe humans are wired for storytelling. It also explains that feeling you get when you "click" with someone.

Before you can connect with your listener, your story must first grab their attention. Some of the best stories start with a tense or dramatic moment. That's because when a listener, viewer or reader anticipates something big is about to happen, their brain releases cortisol, which is known as the fight-or-flight hormone. It makes them alert and ready for what's about to happen. Next, their brain produces oxytocin, and their protective instincts kick in. Also known as the cuddle hormone, oxytocin helps build a bond between storyteller and listener.

At this point, not only are the neurons in your listener's brain mirroring yours, but the listener is also beginning to put themselves in your shoes. Their attitude and intentions are starting to change to reflect yours. The more they become immersed in your story, the more they feel for you. This is called narrative transportation, and it is key to deepening your bond.

But capturing the audience's attention is just the beginning. You've got to continue stimulating their brain if you want to keep them hooked. "Show, don't tell" is considered one of the golden rules of storytelling. It's about engaging as many of your listener's senses as possible. A descriptive story with lots of detail stimulates the brain from start to finish.

It leads to a longer-lasting connection and a better understanding of the information shared. Plus, the listener will retain the information longer.

Stories have the ability to activate several regions of the brain. Each region can be triggered by a specific sense described in the story, as well as when the story itself evokes certain reactions. Consider these regions as you write your Whyography and then again as you edit it. The examples referenced below are from the introduction.

1. WERNICKE'S AND BROCA'S AREA

Wernicke's area and Broca's area are responsible for language processing and comprehension. Spoiler alert: Triggering these parts of the brain is not difficult. They're stimulated by something as complex as a 500-page novel or as simple as a shopping list. String a few sentences together and you've activated these areas of the brain.

2. CEREBELLUM

The cerebellum manages sensory coordination. It's responsible for voluntary muscular activity like speech and sensations of touch, hearing and sight. When your story includes descriptions of touching, sounds or objects, or when it includes dialogue, this region of the brain gets activated.

EXAMPLE: "Listen to the cicadas singing!"

3. SENSORY CORTEX

The sensory cortex manages physical sensations in the body like itches, tickles and throbs. When your story references a physical sensation such as eyes stinging, or it evokes a physical sensation like shivering, this part of the brain is engaged.

EXAMPLE: "Hi, Mom," I said, my eyes stinging with tears.

4. MOTOR CORTEX

The motor cortex manages movement. When your story spurs a movement or physical reaction in the reader, like clenching their fists, it means the motor cortex has been stimulated. References to movement in your story, such as waving to a neighbor, also trigger this part of the brain.

EXAMPLE: They made a clopping noise as she walked through the woods, and as I trailed behind her I often imagined we were on horseback.

5. VISUAL CORTEX

The visual cortex processes and interprets shapes and colors. This region of the brain is activated when your story is presented in a visual format like video, or when it includes images or illustrations. When your story includes detailed descriptions of the landscape or surroundings, the visual cortex is also activated.

EXAMPLE: In spite of the subzero temperatures, the sun was a blazing ball of white light in the cornflower blue sky.

6. OLFACTORY CORTEX

The olfactory cortex processes and interprets scents. When your story refers to bread baking, or freshly cut grass, or any sort of scent—pleasant or unpleasant—it stimulates the olfactory cortex.

EXAMPLE: I'd fill a bucket with as many as I could find, and she'd promise to use my bounty to make campfire coffee cake for breakfast—a mixture of Bisquick, milk, eggs, sugar and berries, poured into a pie tin and baked on an open flame.

7. AUDITORY CORTEX

The auditory cortex receives and processes sounds, voices and music. This region of the brain is activated when your story is presented orally. The auditory cortex is also engaged when your story includes descriptions of sounds.

EXAMPLE: As I sat at my desk working, a murder of crows squawked verbosely outside.

ADDITIONAL CONSIDERATIONS

Stories with data can be tricky. When your audience hears data, only two parts of the brain are stimulated. Remember Wernicke's area and Broca's area? They're the only two that react to data, and it only takes a shopping list for them to get excited. The point here is that as entrepreneurs we can get hyperfocused on data, but it's best to avoid data in storytelling if you want to keep your audience's attention.

If you must include numbers in your story, aim to make them as impactful as possible. For instance, rather than saying 253,000 people were served, you could say more than a quarter of a million people were served. Or you could say two-thirds of program participants passed the test, rather than 32 percent of participants failed the test. Make it about the impact rather than the stats.

Lastly, keep it real. In the prologue I noted how as young adults we begin creating a "story" for ourselves based on what we think the "right people" will want to hear. This facts-first way of thinking influences the information we share throughout our professional career. We're conditioned to elevate the best of the best and bury our failures. As such, you might be inclined to focus only on positive experiences as you develop your Whyography. I'm not suggesting you write a sob story; I am encouraging you to go deeper.

Ask yourself: Are you afraid to be vulnerable and share the messy parts of your story with others? Has your marketing team convinced you that a glossed-up basic business bio is the best way to promote your company? Is your proclivity toward perpetual positivity keeping you from going deeper? A Whyography is designed to honor every aspect of your entrepreneurial journey and what it took to get where you are today—even the parts that were hard. Especially the parts that were hard. Doing so will help you build a genuine connection with your audience.

EXERCISE: WHYOGRAPHY SHITTY FIRST DRAFT

Now that you've started the framework for your Whyography, and you've learned more about the art of storytelling, it's time to move on to your SFD, which stands for shitty first draft. Memoirist Anne Lamott popularized the SFD and said, "All good writers write them. This is how they end up with good second drafts and terrific third drafts." Even before Anne Lamott made the connection, Ernest Hemingway said, "The first draft of anything is shit." The point is that this is the first of what is likely to be several iterations of your story. Multiple drafts are a common part of the writing process. Don't strive for perfection; focus on compiling all the relevant details from your journey.

This process is for writers of every level. Even if you see yourself as more of a business writer, this exercise is designed to help you first get the key points of your journey down. Once you've done that, you'll continue building on the story. In this exercise, you'll transform your bullet points into sentences and expand on important details.

In the example, the bullet points from Lauren's exposition were transformed into sentences. Some additional guidance as you get started:

1. MAKE NEW DRAFTS AND KEEP THE OLD

This is particularly important if you are working electronically. You'll appreciate having drafts of your story at various stages of development to refer back to. The risk of working from a single document is losing details that are important to the story. It's common to delete text that you intend to move to another part of the story or add back later and then neglect to do so. Each time you start a new draft, begin by opening your last draft, selecting "Save As" and entering a new file name.

2. TRANSFORM BULLETS INTO COMPLETE SENTENCES

You'll continue to finesse it as you go, and you may move information from one section to another, but the point now is to add anything you think may be relevant to your story. Include as much detail as possible. Set the scene for your audience. Share specifics about your surroundings and what you were feeling in the moment.

3. WRITE FOR YOURSELF

Right now, your story is for your eyes only. It is perfectly OK (and highly recommended) that you write deep thoughts or dark secrets about your career and entrepreneurial journey that you haven't previously shared. Resist the urge to use bright and shiny marketing language or buzzwords, or to heavily edit yourself. As your Whyography evolves, you'll decide exactly what you want to share in your final draft. Your secrets may ultimately end up on the cutting room floor, but it's important to recognize the part they played in your journey.

4. STICK WITH ONE POINT OF VIEW

As noted earlier, Whyographies are typically written in the third person, which works well for websites and other business materials. Whatever point of view you decide to use, be sure to stick with it throughout the story.

EXAMPLE:

Lauren VanScoy hadn't seen her close girlfriends much since having her second child. While moms with newborns often spend more time with family than socializing, something seemed different about Lauren. She was aware of postpartum depression but hadn't experienced anything like it after the birth of her first child or even in the first few months after her second baby. Then something began to shift. There were signs that things weren't quite right, but she couldn't put her finger on it. She struggled with social anxiety nearly all of the time outside of family conversations. Friends' social media posts and messages were making her feel excluded and even paranoid. Were they leaving her out on purpose? Her friends were concerned, so they invited Lauren to girls' night and started asking questions. Where had she been? Why was she so distant? Was there something she wasn't telling them? The hardest part was that Lauren didn't have any answers and struggled to even speak at all. Then, sitting on her friend's kitchen floor, Lauren had an emotional breakdown.

EXERCISE: WHYOGRAPHY SECOND (THIRD, FOURTH, ETC.) DRAFT

In your next draft, you'll continue filling in and shaping your story. Remember to apply what you learned about the neuroscience of storytelling as you continue building out each of the sections. Paint a picture with words! Make it your goal to activate as many areas of the brain as possible.

As you start this new draft, make a copy of your SFD. Open your SFD, select "Save As" and enter a new file name ("Whyography Second Draft").

The example demonstrates how the exposition section of Lauren's SFD was rearranged slightly and built out further.

EXAMPLE:

Lauren VanScoy was sitting on the kitchen floor of a friend's house having an emotional breakdown. She wanted to be anywhere other than where she was in that moment. She hadn't seen her close girlfriends much since having her second baby several months earlier. But on that "girls' night in," her friends noticed something different about Lauren and were concerned. So they started asking questions. Where had she been? Why was she so distant? Was there something she wasn't telling them? Lauren didn't have any answers. She could barely speak at all.

She knew about postpartum depression but hadn't experienced it after the birth of her first child or even the first few months after her second baby. Now things weren't quite right, but she couldn't put her finger on it. She was struggling with social anxiety. Friends' social media posts were making her feel excluded and even paranoid. She couldn't figure out why it upset her so much, especially since she didn't want to leave the house anyway.

And then there was that moment on her friend's kitchen floor when it all came to a head. While it was incredibly painful at the time, it pushed Lauren to meet with a counselor. As it turned out, there was a medical explanation for what she'd been experiencing—major depressive disorder manifesting as anxiety. She learned about treatment options and worked with her doctor to get her medication right, and her mood improved significantly.

ADDITIONAL CONSIDERATIONS

After you've finished your second draft, set your Whyography aside for a bit. Approach it with fresh eyes later, and be prepared to write a few more drafts.

Some writing experts say it takes seven drafts to get a story to a point where it's ready to move into the editing and proofreading stage. The good news is that you're writing your Whyography, not a full-fledged memoir or business book (at least for now). Your Whyography may not need to be reworked that much, but it will more than likely take more than two drafts.

**DISCOVERING WHAT YOU
DON'T WANT IS JUST AS
IMPORTANT AS FINDING OUT
WHAT YOU DO.**

ELAINE WELTEROTH

INSPIRATION

LINDSEY FROEMMING
FASHION FIX

Lindsey Froemming had recently given birth to a healthy baby girl. She had visions of going back to work at Fashion Fix, her Minnesota-based wardrobe consulting business. After all, her business was her first baby. She had launched it after several friends asked for her expertise as they headed back to work post-maternity leave. They trusted Lindsey's fashion sense—she'd spent nearly a decade as a personal shopper and retail manager for brands like J.Crew, Gap and Loft. For five years, Fashion Fix had thrived. Lindsey was the happiest she had ever been in her career. But everything changed after her daughter arrived.

As a new mom, Lindsey felt depleted and uncomfortable in her own skin. Helping women find styles that made them feel confident while she struggled with her self-esteem felt disingenuous. So Lindsey decided to put the business on hold. Then, nine months after her son was born, something shifted.

"Today is the day," Lindsey said to herself. She was tired of obsessing over her weight. She had struggled with gains and losses before kids, and finding clothes that made her feel good always helped. So she decided to go back to work, make herself her first new client, and document her journey on Instagram. The outcome was exactly as she had hoped. The community she had built rallied around her. New women joined the conversation, sharing their stories. Fashion Fix came to life again, and Lindsey did too.

These days, Lindsey manages motherhood and entrepreneurship like a boss—though she admits she doesn't have it all figured out. One of her secrets is getting out of bed really early, which gives her a solid block of work time. That feeling of productivity sets the tone for her whole day. It allows her to be fully present for her kids when they're awake. She switches back into business mode when they nap and schedules shopping trips in early evening when her husband is home.

Lindsey enjoys working with all her clients, but moms hold a special place in her heart. Whether they are headed back to work or are stay-at-home moms, Lindsey uses tools she's created to educate them on the best shape, fit and fabric for their lifestyle. She is also conscious about price point, so many of her consults take place at Goodwill and other thrift stores. Her motto: "Dress for value, shop for fashion, and feel great every day."

Fashion Fix's mission is to empower women to live their best lives. In addition to styling and shopping services, Lindsey fulfills that mission by sharing the story of her transformation through public speaking, which is where she really comes alive. She makes powerful connections with other women when she shares how she learned to love her body as it is—whether size 8 or 20—and celebrate it with clothes that make her feel good. Lindsey envisions sharing that message with women around the globe.

LISA TABOR
CULTUREBROKERS

The "Purple Rain" movie soundtrack was playing on repeat in Lisa Tabor's head. Her retail management career was relocating her from the East Coast to Minneapolis, Minnesota. The only thing she knew about it was that it was where "Purple Rain" was filmed. And that Prince, the iconic musician who starred in the movie, lived there and was biracial like her. Lisa wanted to feel welcomed and accepted in her new surroundings. Surely the city that brought the world Prince would wrap its arms around her and provide a sense of belonging.

Lisa packed up her life and headed to the Midwest. As she settled in, she began to appreciate what the Twin Cities had to offer. She also realized it was not nearly as culturally diverse as she'd thought it would be. She ended up leaving her job in retail to work for the chamber of commerce and then the convention and visitors bureau in St. Paul. In these roles, she asked business owners how they were making diversity a priority. She learned there were many well-intended companies and leaders that wanted to do so, but they struggled to create environments where a diverse workforce could succeed.

The informal research Lisa conducted sparked a business idea for her. She could educate organizations on the importance of leveraging cultural diversity to create workplaces where everyone could thrive. She hadn't thought about entrepreneurship up to that point, but now friends and colleagues were encouraging her to take the leap. In 2005, Lisa launched CultureBrokers, a consultancy partnering with businesses, nonprofits and government organizations to help them get immediate, measurable and valuable results from their diversity, inclusion and equity efforts.

Lisa developed the Diamond Inclusiveness System to deliver results to her clients. It's a proven formula where diversity plus inclusion times discipline equals equity. The discipline part is where many businesses get stuck. It requires leadership to take a good look at the organization's infrastructure—communications, operations, policies and practices—and consider how each stakeholder group is being served. She provides clients with a two-year road map to achieve results. Her goal is to empower organizations to deliver on promises to staff, customers and the community to build credibility and achieve better business outcomes.

When Lisa started the business, benefit corporations had not yet been established in Minnesota. Her goal for CultureBrokers was to use it as a vehicle for creating a positive impact for workers, the community and society. So she simultaneously established the CultureBrokers Foundation, a nonprofit connected to her business, to ensure her services were accessible and she could bring her bigger vision to life.

Influencing cultural intelligence is energizing for Lisa. She's inspired by organizations that are open-minded about possible solutions and dedicated to making change. "When it comes to diversity and inclusion, it's important to take the time to explore and understand the root issues," she says. "Only then can we create environments where everyone can thrive, regardless of race or culture."

KARLA HEETER
GRACE GEAR

Author's note: This is an edited version of the story Karla Heeter wrote while participating in a Whyography workshop.

"I felt like you never loved me," Karla Heeter confessed to her mother. Her chest was tight, and she fought back tears and nearly choked on the words as they came out. Karla was in her early 50s at the time, but in that moment the wounds of her childhood were real and raw. She'd been raised in a family that never expressed love for one another. There were many times she felt lost, alone and unworthy of love. As she talked with her mom that day—adult to adult—and bared her soul, she hoped for a miracle. She didn't get one. "You were always so obnoxious and overbearing," her mother said. "No one wants to be around that."

Though the conversation was painful, Karla was finally able to focus on healing. That included reflecting on the path her life had taken and focusing on the good that had come from her upbringing. She had developed a deep and loving bond with her childhood best friend—a horse named Julimar. That led her to the Western riding community as an adult, and she even started barrel racing at age 40. She also found what she needed at the local church growing up, which she often attended on her own. She went on to pursue a life of service as an adult, both in her career and through mission work in Guatemala.

It also influenced Karla's entrepreneurial journey. After beating cancer and grieving the loss of a close friend and the tragic deaths of two colleagues, she co-founded the Bounce Back Project with Dr. Corey Martin. It's an organization dedicated to making communities healthier and happier through resilience education. The pair also launched Bounce Travels, which focuses on resilience-centered group excursions.

Then, another business idea began to tug at Karla. She wanted to inspire others to get to know God the way she did. Her faith in God gave her the strength to persevere. She thought about how her Bible and the hope she'd found within it had been with her through the years. She envisioned creating embellished leather-bound Bibles so beautiful their owners would display them prominently on their coffee tables, where they would spark conversations about faith.

In 2017, Karla launched Grace Gear, a company offering extraordinary tools of faith. In addition to handcrafted and custom Bibles, she creates leather Bible covers and journals. She also offers devotionals and bookmarks and sells all of her products online and at select Western events and venues. This venture has enabled Karla to achieve her personal mission to share the unconditional love she found through her relationship with God. Her customers share stories about how the Bibles are starting conversations, just as she hoped. She also donates a portion of Grace Gear's profits to support families in Guatemala.

Through her faith and a lot of self-reflection, Karla came to realize that purpose is often just on the other side of pain. After years of suffering, she was able to accept that her mother did the best she could and to forgive her.

HEIDI MUELLER
EXCELSIOR CANDLE COMPANY

Heidi Mueller was working as an operations manager for a wholesaler, but her passion was designing jewelry from upcycled materials. One day Heidi mentioned to co-workers that she had a meeting with a buyer at a popular boutique after work. On her desk, for all to see, she'd laid out the handmade baubles she'd be bringing to the meeting. Her colleagues gathered around to check out her wares. Suddenly their oohs and aahs were drowned out by men yelling loudly for everyone to step away from their computers. A look beyond the cubicle walls revealed that federal agents had stormed the building and were headed straight for the boss's office.

Heidi hunched down and swiped the earrings and necklaces off her desk and into the bag she'd brought them in. The entire staff was ushered into the cafeteria. Some were singled out for questioning. Hours later, agents demanded everyone go straight to their vehicles without saying a word to one another. Shaken up and still processing what had happened, Heidi drove to the meeting at the boutique as planned—and the buyer bought every single piece in her collection.

That day, Heidi realized how someone else's actions could threaten her livelihood. She had three kids to support and wanted to be in control of her future. Her jewelry business wasn't generating enough profit yet. So she found a new job, and for the next five years she continued to work fulltime while making jewelry in her spare time. When one boutique owner asked if she made candles, it sparked an idea for Heidi. She'd collected plenty of flea market finds—vintage glass and ceramic items—that could be made into candles.

When she started making candles, Heidi realized how much she enjoyed it. She got to use her hands, and she found melting and pouring wax therapeutic. Heidi committed to using the highest-quality ingredients from the start. She formulated her own fragrances from essential oils. She used soy wax, which burns longer and doesn't damage surfaces inside the home. And she used lead-free all-cotton wicks that don't release toxins into the air.

She quickly found candles were a lot more lucrative than jewelry. But as trends changed, demand for shabby chic candleholders diminished. She began sourcing contemporary recycled glass and metal containers from suppliers. She invested in a wax melter and moved operations from her stovetop to her basement. In 2016, she officially launched Excelsior Candle Company and retired her jewelry business.

Today, making hand-poured candles in small batches is Heidi's fulltime job. Her products are available at retailers nationwide. Her commitment to sustainability has not wavered. She encourages customers to bring back their empty Excelsior Candle Company containers for half off their next purchase, and she reuses all of the containers returned to her. She also plans to set up a nonprofit division of the company to help people in need. For now, Heidi gives back by volunteering and supporting other small-business owners every chance she gets.

ALLISON BROSS-WHITE
B. RESALE

Five years after launching b. Resale, her "feel good fashion" boutique, Allison Bross-White received an award acknowledging the success of the business. In an interview about the honor, she spoke of her love of hip-hop music, her passion for clothing design, and her desire to reduce the amount of fast-fashion items clogging up landfills as the inspiration for opening the shop. And then her eyes began to well up with tears. It had become much more than that. With a lump in her throat Allison explained, "I've created a safe haven for people who might not feel comfortable shopping in other stores."

At a young age, Allison began to notice that all things were not created equal. As a teen she started speaking out about the injustices she saw happening around her, and she wanted to make a difference. When she wasn't thinking about how she could change the world, Allison dreamt of launching a nightclub where everyone felt welcomed and accepted. She even began crafting her business plan while she was still in high school.

Her plans evolved over time. After graduating from the Fashion Institute of Design and Merchandising in Los Angeles, California, Allison returned home to Minnesota and started working at the corporate headquarters for Target. The new vision for her own business was now urban resale. In 2010, while she continued to work fulltime, Allison opened the doors to her used clothing store in South Minneapolis. From the start it was different than other thrift shops. Allison is intentional about the items she curates in her boutique. She offers a mix of used, new and locally made goods with a streetwear vibe. The store offers lower price points than most used clothing shops, making it a place where quality fashion is affordable for all. As Allison sees it, everyone should be able to afford a Gucci suit.

Perhaps more importantly, b. Resale provides a different type of shopping experience. Everyone is welcome to shop or just socialize, without being suspected or accused of any wrongdoing. The sign at the front door says, "In our house we believe that Black lives matter, women's rights are human rights, no human is illegal, science is real, love is love, kindness is everything." Allison is proud that her business is defined not by the bottom line, but by how shopping there makes people feel. In fact, if money were no object, she'd gift the shop to an up-and-coming entrepreneur or make everything there free.

Today, b. Resale continues to combine Allison's passions for music, fashion and social justice. The murder of George Floyd happened not far from the shop, and it intensified Allison's commitment to take a stand and use her business to make a difference. Whether it's coordinating supply drives for individuals and organizations in need, encouraging others to vote, or fighting for policy reform, Allison continues to play an active role in supporting the community and advocating for change.

YOUR STORY IS WHAT YOU HAVE, WHAT YOU WILL ALWAYS HAVE. IT IS SOMETHING TO OWN.

MICHELLE OBAMA

PART 6:
THE SUPPER

FOOD FIGHT

"What are you making for dinner?" I asked my dad as we chatted on the phone about Thanksgiving. He and my mom had gotten divorced a few years earlier, when I was 18, and it was the first time he'd be hosting the holiday for my brothers and me. It was also his first time making Thanksgiving dinner. Even so, I knew we weren't having the traditional turkey. My dad only cooked a few things. And turkey wasn't one of them.

"Beef roast?" he suggested. I groaned. I was not a fan of beef roast, but all the men in my family seemed to love it. It was always accompanied by mashed potatoes and peas, which were also my least favorites.

"How about homemade spaghetti?" I suggested.

"Not enough time," he said matter-of-factly.

"Dad, it's Tuesday. Thanksgiving is not for two more days."

He rattled off everything he'd have to do to prepare to make a batch of his homemade sauce. He named several different markets he'd have to go to, all the prep he'd have to do, and the number of hours the sauce would need to simmer. It wasn't logistically possible to do it all in 48 hours, he said.

As I walked through the front door of my dad's house two days later, the smell of roasted pork filled the air. It was a compromise, since I preferred pork to beef. As I made my way to the kitchen, I walked past my brothers, who were lounging in front of the TV watching football. They grunted hello but didn't take their eyes off the game. I was instantly transported back to our childhood.

The dining room table was set with a crisp cotton tablecloth, napkins and sparkling white china. I hadn't recalled seeing the china before and wondered if my dad had always had it. Monogrammed drinking glasses that had been hand-etched by my grandfather flanked each place setting. I hadn't seen those glasses since my parents were still married. At the center of the table sat a vase of flowers and two simple brass candleholders that each held a rose-colored candle. Positioned around the centerpiece were platters of sliced meat, potatoes, vegetables and bread.

"Wow!" I said as I greeted my dad. "This is fancy!"

We typically ate supper at the table, but there'd never been a tablecloth, fine china or flowers before. Since it was a new era, and a holiday, my dad said he thought we'd have a civilized meal. The presentation definitely took things up a notch. Within minutes we were all seated around the table, making small talk and passing platters of food.

"Save some food for the rest of us," my younger brother said to my older brother, who was filling his plate with generous portions of everything.

"No Negative Nancys on Thanksgiving," I said, sounding more like the oldest than the middle sibling. "Eating is the whole point of Thanksgiving."

My younger brother continued to poke at my older brother.

"Stop it," I said firmly. Now I was annoyed.

My younger brother kept at it, and my older brother ignored the jabs for a minute or two. And then suddenly they were both shouting at the top of their lungs. Bickering wasn't new for them. They'd been doing it for decades. But they'd never had an argument this heated at the dinner table. And certainly not on Thanksgiving.

"No Negative Nancys!" I said again, this time shouting over them.

They continued to lob insults at each other. The volume of their voices continued to rise. Potatoes flew through the air. A plate ended up on the floor.

"Knock it off!" my dad shouted. "Or this will be the last time I invite you to Thanksgiving dinner!"

Finally, my brothers went mute. I stepped outside to get some air. After I came back in, we finished eating in silence. There was no lingering at the table after dinner and no watching more football. It was the shortest Thanksgiving dinner in our family history.

A few days later, my dad and I talked on the phone about what had happened. "The table looked amazing," I said. "Too bad about the food fight."

"It's a good thing we didn't have spaghetti!" my dad said, laughing.

It left me longing for the spaghetti suppers of my childhood, where we all just served ourselves right from the pot and then sat around the table eating and talking.

For years, when I told the story about that first Thanksgiving dinner hosted by my dad, I left out the part about my brothers' food fight and how we barely spoke for the rest of the meal. I'd delight in sharing how my dad made pork instead of turkey. I'd wax poetic about being served a delicious feast at a fancy table. I was embarrassed by how my brothers behaved that day. I was ashamed to admit my family's dysfunction and feared I'd be judged for their behavior. So, I edited the story and romanticized it. I revised history to make it what I thought would be more respectable.

At some point, as I got older, I realized more people could probably relate to what had really taken place that Thanksgiving than to the fairy-tale version of my story. I don't recall when the shift happened or what prompted it—maybe someone shared a crazy holiday story and I decided there was no reason not to share mine. What I do know is that my family isn't perfect. Nobody's is. I'm not perfect either. My flaws are what make me human. And one of the best things about storytelling is its ability to build genuine and powerful human connections between the storyteller and the audience.

WE CAN DO ANYTHING WE WANT IF WE STICK TO IT LONG ENOUGH.

HELEN KELLER

INSTRUCTION

EDITING AND PROOFREADING

You've reached the point in the Whyography process where you'll think about what you'd like to bring to the table. Are you going to plop a big ol' pot of sauce down on the table and invite everyone to serve themselves? Or will you present it at a beautifully set table on your best dinnerware? What about your portions? Generous? Conservative? Somewhere in the middle? Once you've completed your third our fourth draft—the version you think is close to final—you'll need to review it with an editor's eye to determine how you want to serve it up.

LESSON: WHAT YOU BRING TO THE TABLE (EDITING)

You've been slowly editing your Whyography with each of your drafts. Now you'll dig in a bit more and decide which details are most important to include in your story. Since you've been writing for yourself up to this point, consider whether there are parts of your journey that may not be relevant or that you'd rather not share with the world. As you work, be sure to make new drafts and keep earlier versions. You'll appreciate having your drafts to refer back to—if only for yourself. When you edit from a single document you risk losing details you may need later. Begin by opening your last draft, selecting "Save As" and entering a new file name. For this version, save a copy as "Whyography" and the date (e.g., "Whyography MM-DD-YY"). Save it with a new date each time you edit it.

Once you've reviewed it and removed any details you deemed unnecessary to the story, begin reading through your document again and use these editing tips.

1. CHECK YOUR POINT OF VIEW

Is the narrator's point of view in your Whyography consistent throughout? Switching point of view is like inviting guests to join you for a black-tie dinner and then serving Spaghetti-Os. It can be confusing to the audience. Decide whether you'll write in first person or third person and stick with it.

2. ELIMINATE THE NEGATIVE

As you read through your Whyography, check your tone to ensure you're using a positive voice when possible. When it makes sense, instead of saying what something wasn't, say what it was. Look for sentences with words like don't, won't, shouldn't, etc. and challenge yourself to write the sentence again without using not. For example, rather than saying "I didn't know what to do," you could say "I wondered what to do."

3. KEEP IT REAL

I know, I know. I just said keep it positive. Sometimes positive can be negative—like the use of bright and shiny marketing language or buzzwords. Consumers are smarter than ever. Those glossed-up bullet points in a basic business bio are not what impress or connect with them. My motto: keep it real or keep it to yourself. Speaking of keeping it real, I encourage you to be brave and include the messy parts of your entrepreneurial journey—even if they feel like a downer.

4. GET THE LENGTH RIGHT

Sentence length is a lot like the time you spend with family on Thanksgiving. Too short and it may leave you wanting more. Too long and it may get on your nerves or leave you bored out of your mind (or maybe just overly stuffed and ready for a nap). Pay attention to sentences that are particularly long. Even if the sentence is grammatically correct, your audience may lose interest. For sentences that contain more than one thought, try dividing them into two succinct sentences.

5. AVOID REDUNDANCIES

Redundancies are common in writing, and they're often overlooked. There might be instances when it's important to reiterate a thought to make a point—like my Thanksgiving plea for no negativity. As you edit your Whyography, be on the lookout for repetition. Have you intentionally shared the same thought more than once? Is it really necessary to do so? Consider combining similar thoughts in one sentence or deleting one of the duplicative sentences.

6. AVOID THE UNNECESSARY

Just as a food fight is unnecessary on Thanksgiving, some words might be unnecessary in your Whyography. If you tend to use words like "really," "basically," "definitely," actually" and "generally," consider omitting them to make your sentence clearer. And "that" is a word that is not needed nearly as often as it is used. Or "that" is a word not needed nearly as often as it is used. (See what I did there?) Consider whether you really need it as often as you've used it in your Whyography.

LESSON: SETTING THE TABLE (PROOFREADING)

Whether you're serving a family-style Thanksgiving dinner or an all-you-can-eat spaghetti buffet, setting the table goes beyond the food and flatware. There are many additional details to consider. Are there enough places to sit? Have the glasses been checked for spots and filled? Are the condiments on the table? These last details before everyone sits down to enjoy the feast are the equivalent of proofreading. Once you've pared down your Whyography and completed your edits, proofreading can begin.

This is the final step in writing your Whyography. Proofreading is searching your writing for errors before you publish your work. It can be helpful to break down proofreading into phases and spread them out over time.

1. STEP AWAY FOR A WHILE

Wait a day or two, a week, or even a month before you begin proofreading. Taking a break will allow you to look at your document with fresh eyes.

2. LIST YOUR COMMON MISTAKES

We all have a pattern of mistakes we make when writing. Perhaps you consistently use the wrong spelling for a certain word. Or maybe you aren't great with punctuation. Creating a list of mistakes you commonly make will help you focus.

3. PRINT A HARD COPY

Reading on a computer screen is not an ideal way to proofread. Having a hard copy you can mark up with a pen is a more effective approach. It can also be really satisfying.

4. REFORMAT YOUR DOCUMENT

It's typical to overlook errors when you read the same document over and over—and chances are you've probably been looking at your Whyography formatted the same way for weeks. Before you print it and dig in, change the font type and size, as well as the margins. It'll allow you to see things you may have missed previously.

5. SLOW DOWN

Many mistakes in writing occur when we rush. Reading slowly and intentionally will give your eyes enough time to spot errors.

6. READ IT ALOUD

Reading out loud helps you to notice run-on sentences, awkward transitions, and other grammatical and organizational issues you may not notice when reading silently. There are three ways to do this: read aloud to yourself, read aloud to a friend or family member, or have a friend or family member read aloud to you while you just listen.

7. BEGIN AT THE END

Read individual sentences one at a time starting from the end of your Whyography rather than the beginning. This forces you to pay attention to the sentence itself rather than to your Whyography as a whole.

8. USE ONLINE RESOURCES

There are valuable resources available online for checking grammar and punctuation, including www.grammarcheck.net/editor and www.grammarly.com, which offer free online grammar checking. (These sites also offer upgrades that require a fee.)

9. ENLIST THE HELP OF FRIENDS AND FAMILY

This is sometimes referred to as "alpha reading." Have someone you trust look at your Whyography after you have made all of your edits. A new reader will be able to help you catch mistakes you might have overlooked.

10. PARTNER WITH AN EXPERT

In the publishing world, this is sometimes referred to as "beta reading." After editing and proofreading on your own, or with the help of friends and family, if your Whyography is in need of support, working with an editor might be beneficial. They can help you polish your story and get it ready to share with the world.

IF I WAITED FOR PERFECTION, I
WOULD NEVER WRITE A WORD.

MARGARET ATWOOD

INSPIRATION

JACQUIE BERGLUND
FINNEGANS

Jacquie Berglund sat mesmerized by the keynote speaker on stage in front of her. It was Bill Shore, founder of Share Our Strength, a national nonprofit dedicated to ending childhood hunger, and he'd just said the smartest thing she had ever heard. As he shared his lifelong work influencing social change, he spoke about for-profit companies funding their own nonprofit activities to solve society's problems. It was the late 1990s and the first time Jacquie had heard the concept of social entrepreneurship. She had a lightbulb moment so powerful she felt like her hair was on fire.

Jacquie had returned to her home state of Minnesota just a few years earlier, after getting a master's degree in international relations in Paris and working in international economic development in Moscow, where she saw the power of entrepreneurship in action. Now back home, she was working as marketing director for Minnesota restaurateur Kieran Folliard when she heard Bill Shore speak, and she was so inspired she proposed to Kieran that they launch a new concept: their own craft beer with a mission. She envisioned money from beer sales helping to alleviate hunger in the Midwest. She and Kieran partnered with a local brewery and brought Jacquie's vision to life, offering Kieran's Irish Ale in all three of his restaurants.

Jacquie was so passionate about this new venture that she took her biggest risk yet: She quit her marketing gig and sold everything she owned to pursue social entrepreneurship full time. She bought Kieran out of his half of the beer business (for a dollar at his insistence), changed the name to FINNEGANS and began expanding its market. Soon she was raising thousands of dollars each year to help feed the hungry in Minnesota and beyond. She was turning beer into food.

In 2017, Jacquie took the concept of paying it forward to the next level by creating the FINNOVATION Lab, a business incubator that offers programming to help social enterprises launch, scale and increase their impact. The nine-month FINNOVATION Fellowship supports early-stage entrepreneurs who have bold ideas for sustainable, systems-level change.

FINNEGANS House, a dedicated multi functional space in downtown Minneapolis developed in partnership with local builder Kraus Anderson, opened in 2018. Having a physical building has enabled Jacquie to take her vision for FINNEGANS to the next level by brewing and canning on-site. It also features a taproom for serving the public, plus spaces for meetings and events.

More than $1.8 million has been raised through partnerships, events and FINNEGANS beer sales. Jacquie is not just a pioneer of the giveback business concept in Minnesota. She has built the second-longest-running social enterprise in the country donating 100 percent of its profits to help solve a societal problem—second only to Newman's Own. She remains committed to demonstrating the true power of for-profit companies funding their own nonprofit ventures to make the kind of impact they imagine in the world.

LINDSEY RAMUNDT
COACH LINDSEY BETH

Lindsey Ramundt was on her way to the gym, and her stomach was in knots. Just the thought of walking into the building made her anxious. In fact, everything about the gym was terrifying. She had gained and lost weight over the years, and her recent pregnancy had exacerbated that. Losing weight this time seemed daunting, and when things got hard, Lindsey often gave up. On this day, she was determined things would be different. And then, as she thought about being judged at the gym, Lindsey threw up in the car.

A few weeks earlier, Lindsey had been looking through images on her phone. Instagram had recently launched, and she was curious how photos of her son might look using the filters. But after she downloaded the app, rather than posting her own images, she found herself checking out hashtags that seemed interesting—particularly those that included the word "transformation." That's when she stumbled on an account belonging to a woman who had used weightlifting to transform her body.

Before that, Lindsey had never considered weightlifting. Something was different this time. A physical transformation was appealing, but it was more than that. Lindsey felt a desire for a total life transformation, in a way she'd never experienced before. It was strong enough to motivate her to start weightlifting, which she did, despite vomiting on the way to the gym that first day.

Little by little, weightlifting did transform Lindsey's life. She eventually experienced a complete shift from who she'd been previously. She started doing things that were hard and actually enjoyed it. And when one of the most difficult things she could imagine happened—her marriage ended—fitness was Lindsey's lifeline.

Lindsey ended up moving across the country from Texas to Minnesota. Now a single mom, she needed to go back to work. She took a variety of jobs to make ends meet, but she kept gravitating toward fitness-related work. It started when an acquaintance asked for her help opening a gym and culminated with a fulltime position with a wearable fitness device company.

While she loves all things fitness, weightlifting remains Lindsey's passion. It inspired her to get her personal training certification and launch her personal training business. She is committed to helping women become less intimidated by weightlifting and improve their overall health. Every session includes a fitness, nutrition and mindset component, and her program is delivered through an app, so it's available anytime for busy women.

Beyond helping them achieve better health with the app, Lindsey is creating a community where women can feel empowered. Her program includes a Facebook group, where she provides live trainings and tips to help members stay focused on their goals. For Lindsey, weightlifting has transformed her interior even more than her exterior, and that's what she wants to do for her clients. "I want women to have that internal transformation they didn't even know they needed, like I did."

TWILA DANG
MATRIARCH DIGITAL MEDIA

Twila Dang made a joke during a lunch with a group of new friends about how great it would be if someone paid her to talk for a living. One of the friends happened to work in radio and connected Twila to her boss, who—after learning about her blog on pop culture and parenting—offered Twila a job. Up to that point, she'd been working in what she considered the best job she'd ever had as a stay-at-home mom. Now her kids were getting older and needed her less. She was ready to start a new career as a talk show host. And Twila was on top of the world.

As a professional woman reentering the workforce, Twila saw the world through a whole new lens. She started to notice something that didn't sit well with her. There was a recurring message in mainstream media aimed at her demographic, saying that women in their 40s were losing or had lost their appeal and relevance. They needed to change who they were to fit in. Twila didn't see it that way. She was the best she'd ever been. Not only did she want to continue sharing her voice with the world, but she wanted other women like her to have the same opportunity.

So Twila focused on honing her broadcasting skills. She mastered using production equipment. She became adept at doing research, organizing information, interviewing guests, managing the clock and telling stories. And she considered ways to create media for women like her. Then, as she was co-hosting a Sunday radio program with Dr. Eric Heegaard, an obstetrician-gynecologist, she shared the seed of an idea for a podcast network to amplify the voices of all women. Not only did he encourage her to do it, but he said he'd invest.

In 2017, with an initial investment from Dr. Heegaard, Matriarch Digital Media was born. The Minneapolis, Minnesota-based podcast network honors women at whatever stage of life they're in. Through a variety of programming and "Women in Podcasting" events, Twila aims to make women feel understood, encouraged and uplifted. Programs address topics like body positivity, motherhood and entrepreneurship. In addition to creative directing and executive producing, Twila co-hosts "Twila and Natalie," which addresses life for women over 40, and a podcast with Dr. Heegaard called "Gynocast."

Twila is energized by the continued momentum of the podcasting industry and believes it's a powerful medium for connecting. She hopes women who listen to her programs feel like they're hanging out with their best friends. But her overall vision is much bigger. Twila wants to influence the way the world communicates to and about women and girls. She wants every woman to know: "You are amazing and wonderful just as you are."

Twila still believes motherhood is the best job she's ever had, but her business takes a close second. For the first time in her life, she feels like she is doing the professional work she was meant to do.

KYLEE LEONETTI
LEONETTI CONFETTI

Kylee Leonetti was at a business meeting to talk about her video and photography services. Her thoughts drifted as she learned more about the organization she was meeting with, Wayside Recovery Center, which was dedicated to supporting women and their families through recovery from substance abuse. She had a flashback of a fellow waitress she worked with many years earlier, who had slipped her the number to Narcotics Anonymous on a tiny piece of paper. With a sweet Southern accent and a look of genuine concern, she'd said, "Sugar, I don't know you all that well, but I think you need help." As Kylee thought of that long-ago moment, she remembered that feeling, like she'd been exposed for the whole world to see and the wind had been knocked out of her. Goosebumps rose on Kylee's arms.

That interaction had transformed Kylee's life forever—she went to Narcotics Anonymous and finally felt seen and heard and hopeful. And in that business meeting years later it hit her like a freight train: She could help other women in recovery. Kylee and her husband, Christian, had been working together for years, bringing stories to life for organizations with their film, photo and production company. It was what brought her to the meeting with Wayside Recovery Center in the first place. In that moment, Kylee knew she could have a greater impact. And she felt strongly that it might be her purpose to do so.

A year earlier, Kylee had quietly started another business, making confetti by hand. It began as a way to add color and whimsy to her photo shoots, but it quickly became more than a fun parttime project. When a Minnesota tourism agency wanted gallons of bright yellow confetti for an interactive exhibit on display during Super Bowl 52, Kylee's side hustle started to gain momentum on Instagram.

As demand increased, she knew she'd need more workers to create her hand-cut confetti. So Kylee connected the dots. The women of Wayside Recovery needed something to focus on as they got sober. Even more, they needed someone to trust and believe in them. Kylee proposed a partnership with the organization—she would provide employment experience, some extra cash, and a bridge for women leaving addiction so they could cross into their new sober lives with a greater sense of purpose.

In 2018, Leonetti Confetti launched officially, exclusively employing the women of Wayside. They mix perfectly portioned confetti packets, wands and poppers in custom color combinations for weddings and parties. Bulk confetti is available for bigger events as well.

Kylee describes Leonetti Confetti as an experience of full-circle joy: From the moment you place an order, you're making an impact in the lives of the women who create the confetti for your next party or event. You celebrate them, and they celebrate YOU.

KIM WITCZAK
WOODY MATTERS

Kim Witczak's job required her to travel all over the world to work on film and photo shoots for big brands. A business trip in 2003 should've been like the others. However, before she left, her typically laid-back husband, Woody, wasn't himself. He'd landed his dream job but wasn't sleeping. A month earlier, he was prescribed Zoloft, an antidepressant. He wasn't depressed and didn't have a history of depression, but his physician said it would take the edge off and help him sleep. A week before her trip, Woody fell to the kitchen floor clutching his head and begging Kim to help him. They called the doctor, who said it would take time for the drug to kick in. Now Kim was working 700 miles from home, and Woody wasn't responding to messages. She asked her dad to check on him, and when he called back, the news was something she never imagined. Woody had taken his own life at 37 years old.

In an instant, Kim's world came crashing down. As she scrambled to get home, her brother-in-law began researching antidepressants and suicide. He learned about Food and Drug Administration (FDA) hearings regarding a link between Prozac and suicide. Drug makers were ordered to do a study, but it was more than a decade later and no black box warning (BBW) had been issued about serious potential adverse reactions to antidepressants. When the coroner suggested Zoloft may have had something to do with Woody's suicide, Kim made it her mission to get to the bottom of it.

She worked with an attorney to file a wrongful death lawsuit in federal court. She sat in on hearings in Washington, D.C., and learned about drug laws. She became the voice of the voiceless, speaking out for Woody and others who'd lost their lives as unwitting drug company test subjects. She launched Woody Matters, an organization dedicated to educating consumers, advocating for patients and families, and influencing drug safety reform.

In 2004, the FDA finally issued a BBW regarding the increased risk of suicidality in children using antidepressants. Two years later, the warning was extended to include teens and young adults. Meanwhile, Kim's legal team gained access to reams of sealed documents from the makers of Zoloft confirming they knew about the suicide risk and kept it secret. The case was settled out of court. And as Kim saw the inner workings of the American health care system, she realized the extent of its brokenness. It fueled her to keep fighting for change.

Today, thanks to the efforts of Kim and others, change is slowly happening. Consumers are getting smarter. Laws are being enacted to protect people. And there is always more work to do. If Kim ever doubts the difference one person can make when taking on a giant industry, she reminds herself of a time when a media conglomerate proposed a second cell phone tower near her and Woody's home, and Woody decided to fight it. She asked if it would be worth the effort, and he said: "I'd rather try like hell and lose than do nothing at all." The request to build the tower was denied. And Woody's words are now the mantra that guides Kim every day.

YOU GAIN STRENGTH,
COURAGE AND CONFIDENCE
BY EVERY EXPERIENCE IN
WHICH YOU REALLY STOP TO
LOOK FEAR IN THE FACE.

ELEANOR ROOSEVELT

PART 7:
THE STORYTELLER

EVEN IF YOU WOBBLE

I sat frozen in my car, parked in the lot of the Minneapolis museum where I was working at the time. While temps in Minnesota often dip into the negative double digits during winter, this was an especially warm fall day. The temperature outside had nothing to do with my inability to move or my fitful shaking. On that sunny October morning, still buckled into the driver's seat, I was having a full-blown panic attack. Just seconds earlier, I had looked in the rearview mirror and caught a glimpse of my hair.

After my cancer diagnosis and surgery, I had taken my impending chemo-induced hair loss like a champ. Even before I started treatment, I had a head-shaving celebration with a couple of close friends, and I donated 10-plus inches of my bottle-blonde hair to a nonprofit that makes wigs for kids with cancer. I purchased a really great wig for myself. It looked a lot like it was my real hair if my real hair had ever been a dark chocolate brown inverted bob. Unfortunately, I had to stop wearing it a few weeks later when I developed a rash on my tender bald scalp from all the steroids I was prescribed. Steroid folliculitis. Don't Google it. I switched to hats and never looked back.

I finally started to sprout peach fuzz at summer's end, and I was ecstatic. By October, I had a full head of super-short light brown hair. At first, I loved it. I was so happy it was back. It was so low-maintenance. Every morning I'd step out of the shower and give it a shake, and it somehow dried itself into a mini faux-hawk. I soon realized that what was a stylish look for David Beckham, P!nk or a 6-foot-tall supermodel wasn't quite working for me. Especially when I was regularly being mistaken for a 12-year-old boy. I decided it was time to splurge and treat myself to a salon day.

Sitting in the stylist's chair felt empowering, like a post-cancer rite of passage. I realized it had been over a year since I had the full salon experience—putting on a gown, sipping sparkling water, paging through gossip magazines, eavesdropping on the chitchat going on around me. I'd forgotten how wonderful the head and neck massage is. I had no recollection of how much time is needed to complete this beauty regimen. I'd forgotten how important it is to do nice things for myself.

Three hours and $300 later, I had a new cut and color I was pretty sure was fabulous. I left the salon and headed to the mall, spending hundreds more on a new dress and boots to wear to a friend's birthday party that evening. I justified the investment by telling myself, "You can't put a price tag on feeling whole again." I didn't exactly feel whole, but I felt a little more like the person I was before cancer.

Those feelings flew out the window the second I saw the party photos posted on social media. The comments said I looked fabulous, but I saw a freak with a frumpy haircut and an ill-fitting dress. A disfigured monster created by the toxic chemicals that were meant to kill my disease. Too ugly to be seen in public.

The monster first reared its ugly head a few months earlier, while I was in the midst of cancer treatment. On a steamy summer evening, as I lay on my sofa recovering from an eight-hour chemotherapy session, an unsuspecting middle school-aged boy came to my house selling candy bars. He froze in terror as I opened the door and revealed my rashy bald head. I had no energy and could barely speak. The monster rendered him speechless.

Soon the monster was holding me hostage in my home, urging me to stay indoors until my hair grew back. After eight weeks of medical leave, when I went back to work, the monster followed. Speaking publicly was something I'd done often throughout my career, and it had previously been a piece of cake. Thanks to the monster, the mere thought of it had become excruciating. I often found myself at a loss for words and unable to think quickly on my feet. When I did speak, my voice would shake. The monster would ridicule me.

I'd been working with a therapist who'd revealed the monster's identity: social anxiety. She'd been teaching me mindfulness meditation to help regulate my thoughts, manage my emotions, and make the monster disappear. On this particular day at the museum, as the monster held me captive in the parking lot, none of the practices I learned in therapy seemed to be working.

Then, as I spotted a white van emblazoned with a television station logo pulling into the lot, the monster began to lose its grip. The host of a local TV talk show was coming to film a segment about an exhibit. I was scheduled to give him a guided tour and appear on camera. "You can do this," I said aloud, practicing positive self-talk.

Like a stubborn cube of ice that was finally melty enough to pop out of its tray, I ejected myself from the car. I slung my bag on my shoulder and tugged at the hem of my dress to make sure it wasn't clinging to my tights. My head felt light, and for a moment I wondered if I might faint.

"You can do this. You can do this. You can do this," I told myself. "You've done this hundreds of times. You're good at this. You're great at this."

"Are you sure you're great at it?" the monster asked.

As the talk show host and camera operator stepped out of the TV van and walked toward the museum, I picked up my pace to catch up.

"Hello!" I called after them, my voice quivering. "I'm Chris—I'll be giving you a tour today."

"Or maybe you won't," the monster said.

I forced a smile and felt crimson bloom over my cheeks. My ears pulsed with heat, and my heart thumped rapidly against my chest. I drew a long breath in through my nose, paused for a second, and then pushed the air out through my mouth. Then suddenly, for no apparent reason, I tripped. There wasn't an untied shoelace, a bit of loose gravel or a single curb to blame. In fact, I was barely even moving. Fucking monster. I stumbled briefly but managed to stay upright.

"You OK?" the camera guy asked.

"Oh, yeah," I assured him. "I'm like a Weeble."

The camera guy laughed. I waited for the monster to say something. Nothing.

"A Weeble?" the TV host asked.

"You know, those little plastic egg-shaped toys," the camera operator said. "Weebles wobble but they don't fall down."

We all laughed. I listened again for the monster. The only thing I heard was the camera guy as he talked about blooper reels of reporters tripping on camera. We walked through the museum and continued to chat. They asked me if I'd done a segment like this before. I shared that I'd done dozens of them, but it was my first on-camera appearance since kicking cancer's ass and I was a little rusty. They joked that it was like riding a bike. They reminded me it was a recorded segment. If anything sucked, it could be edited out later. When the camera was finally turned on, we just continued talking casually, as we had been previously. The monster was nowhere to be found.

When I watched the talk show segment that aired later that week, I saw no trace of the disfigured monster I'd seen in the mirror the morning of the taping. I saw a woman who was a little rusty at public speaking. I witnessed someone making a comeback. A strong woman who'd beaten a deadly disease. Someone whose hair was growing back and whose scars were healing. A perfectly imperfect human being. Sometimes her voice shook when she spoke. Occasionally she wobbled. And sometimes she even fell down. She always managed to get back up again.

INSTRUCTION

CONFIDENTLY COMMUNICATE

Now is the time to fully own your story and honor all you've gone through to get where you are today. For the record, when I say "own your story," I'm referring to more than an ability to share stories via carefully crafted messages and images on social media. Of course, what you present on social media is important, but you also have to get comfortable stepping out from behind your computer or mobile device to truly master talking about your business in a number of different real-life scenarios.

If you struggle to talk about your business publicly, you're not alone. Female-identifying entrepreneurs face a number of obstacles, and many things influence our ability to communicate with confidence. Having worked with thousands of women leaders and business owners to hone their public relations and speaking efforts, I can say for certain that confident communicators embrace three important strategies: They recognize fear for what it is and use it as a tool; they reject gender and cultural biases as the "norm"; and they understand that being confident in who they are requires knowing what they stand for.

LESSON: USE FEAR AS A TOOL

To overcome fear, it helps to first understand what happens to your brain when you're afraid. Scientists believe the human brain is like three in one. Your reptilian brain is responsible for primitive drives like thirst, hunger, sex, and establishing and guarding your turf. Your old mammal brain is in charge of memory, motivation and emotions. And your new mammal brain is responsible for language, reasoning and planning.

Fear is basically your reptilian brain telling you it perceives a threat. This has long been critical to our survival. When our cave-dwelling ancestors encountered a saber-toothed tiger, their reptilian brain screamed, "You're going to die!" It sparked a physical reaction to tackle the tiger, run like hell, or hide in a cave until the coast was clear.

While the human brain has evolved, our initial reaction to a perceived threat is still fight or flight. The good news is that at some point our advanced new mammal brain typically takes over to assess a threat and make a rational decision about what to do next. The bad news is that sometimes we get stuck in our reptilian brain. And these days, it's not just the threat of a tiger that can stop us in our tracks. A threat to our social structure can evoke the same reaction. In my case, my reptilian brain perceived work-related challenges as an actual threat to my life. On the day the TV crew was scheduled to tour the museum, my first response was to hide in a cave.

This can happen to anyone at any time. It happens to even the most confident of communicators preparing to face an audience of one or one thousand. It's not an abnormal reaction; it's how humans are wired. The key is recognizing it and developing new habits to get out of your primitive brain. Here are a few ways how:

1. IDENTIFY AND ACKNOWLEDGE YOUR FEAR

Identifying what you're afraid of is a necessary first step in conquering your fear. The next time you're preparing to speak in public and your nerves are getting the best of you, ask yourself, "What am I really afraid of?" Take some time to journal about it, write it on a Post-it, or simply say it out loud. Then, remind yourself that fear is a signal from your reptilian brain, which is just trying to keep you safe. Acknowledge and address it directly. "Hey Lizzie Lizard Brain, I appreciate the heads-up, but pitching my business to a potential investor is not life-threatening. In fact, it's an amazing opportunity to get much-needed resources to grow my company. So, thank you for your service, but I've got this." Or you could just tell the ol' reptile to scram.

2. TAKE A BREATH

Sometimes in the moment, when fear strikes, it can be tricky to identify your fear and make a logical decision about what to do next. Get into the habit of shifting your focus from your mind to your body—and specifically your breathing. As you start to panic, try the four-seven-eight breathing technique. Inhale deeply through your nose for four seconds, hold your breath for seven seconds, and exhale through your mouth for eight seconds. If you can't remember the timing, make up your own. Focus on counting and the physical act of taking air into your lungs and releasing it. Repeat the process a few times until your head is clear. With practice, your first reaction to fear will be to just breathe.

3. GET COMFORTABLE BEING UNCOMFORTABLE

It's human nature to choose comfort and to surround yourself with all that is soft, safe and secure. But breakthroughs and aha moments rarely come from inside comfort zones. Make a weekly habit of doing something that scares you. Designate "Scary Saturdays" as the day to try out a new cuisine, introduce yourself to someone you've been dying to meet, or sign up for an event you keep talking yourself out of. Rather than making your weekly challenge about facing your biggest fears, focus on facing something you continually avoid because it makes you uncomfortable. The more you take small steps out of your comfort zone, the more courageous you become. Soon you'll be tackling the unknown head-on without hesitation.

LESSON: CHALLENGE THE STATUS QUO

While overcoming fear is an important part of mastering confident communications, female founders are also working to slay a bigger monster—the gender and cultural biases that threaten our livelihood. Fighting for equality is a constant battle. If we want to see changes in our lifetime, we must continue to challenge the status quo. A great place to start is advocating for the rights of at least one woman—you. You've got to get comfortable using your voice and claiming the recognition you deserve.

In my home state, the residents are often described as "Minnesota Nice." For some, this refers to a certain level of politeness or reservedness in public. Ask many Minnesotans how they're doing, and regardless of circumstances they're likely to respond, "Fine." For women entrepreneurs in Minnesota, it often translates to a hesitance to share our successes. Or to talk about them at all. I've observed this firsthand with many of the women who attend Whyography workshops.

This reluctance to tout professional achievements extends far beyond Minnesota. Studies reveal that women across the country feel uncomfortable with self-promotion. It starts at a young age. Girls are conditioned to be "nice" and get good grades. We become accustomed to measuring our worth with high marks in school and an ability to follow the rules. This mindset stays with us as we enter the workforce. However, in professional environments, doing what you're told, keeping your head down, and working hard are not enough. Your work no longer speaks for itself—you have to speak for it.

The bottom line is that a hesitancy to self-promote significantly limits success. It robs women of resources and opportunities. From a funding standpoint, female founders receive less than a quarter of small-business bank loans and less than 3 percent of venture capital. And those numbers decrease significantly for women of color. One big reason men receive more funding is because they're not afraid to ask for it. They have no qualms talking about their track record. They confidently communicate their purpose and impact. Take a page from the playbook of male entrepreneurs and develop these skill sets:

1. LEARN TO EMBRACE FAILURE

No one likes to fail, but women are more likely than men to internalize feelings about mistakes, setbacks, and failures, and to then get stuck. Men don't typically let past failures keep them from pursuing future opportunities, but many women do. It's high time we stop beating ourselves up and spinning our wheels. The most powerful lessons come from failure. So use failure as your motivation to move forward. There's no shame in changing direction based on new information. Take a step back, ask yourself what you learned, and pinpoint what to do differently next time. Embracing failure as part of the process for growth is how to get comfortable taking bigger risks in the future.

2. CELEBRATE YOUR STRENGTHS

As women, we are often our own worst critics, focusing on weaknesses rather than the best parts of ourselves. This is largely because women believe if we concentrate on our weaknesses, we can change them. Research shows we actually grow faster when we focus on improving our strengths. Earlier in this process, you collected feedback from others regarding some of the specific strengths you'd bring to a survival situation. The responses you received are invaluable. Not only do they reveal your strengths, but they demonstrate how highly others regard you. Refer back to the list if self-doubt creeps in. Better yet, post it on your office wall. Never forget that your talents, gifts and strengths are unique to you. No one else can do what you do the way you do it.

3. LET GO OF PERFECT

Women are more likely than men to be perfectionists. For many women, people-pleasing in adolescence manifests as perfectionism in adulthood.

We tend to compare ourselves to other women (and men) and worry that we're not smart enough, not experienced enough, not credentialed enough, not worthy enough—the list goes on. While the struggle to feel like enough is not exclusive to women, men are less likely to get wrapped up in these thoughts. It's time to let go of perfect and embrace "good enough." Reevaluate your standards and relax them. Switch up your vocabulary and replace "should" with "could." And don't forget, you're human.

LESSON: KNOW WHAT YOU STAND FOR

Through the Whyography process, you've taken a closer look at the combination of your upbringing, values, personality and strengths, and how they make you uniquely you. You've identified people and events that influenced the person you are today. You've made connections between significant moments in your life and how your values and strengths inspired you to take action. All of this helped reveal what you stand for, and it informed your WHY.

Glinda the Good Witch told Dorothy in "The Wizard of Oz," "You've always had the power, my dear. You just had to learn it for yourself." The power you've discovered is your WHY. Now you've got your very own pair of jewel-encrusted magic shoes. Ruby slippers equipped with a special kind of GPS that always points you in the direction of your purpose. When the future seems uncertain or you feel lost, the shoes will right you and give you the power to keep moving forward.

This power—solidly knowing your WHY—is one of the best natural confidence boosters there is. You're working hard to center your business around it. You've begun crafting key business messaging with your WHY. This goes a long way toward confident communications.

Here are some important practices to help you continue to cultivate confidence:

1. LEAD WITH YOUR WHY

Let potential partners, employees, contractors and consultants know your WHY before you start working together, in order to ensure you're on the same page. Don't compromise your values by working with individuals and organizations not aligned with your WHY. Review your WHY Statement daily. Make it your mantra. Get comfortable with your Pitch on Purpose. Practice it until it rolls effortlessly off your tongue. Earlier in this process, you made connections between major life moments, how your values and strengths propelled you to take action, and the result. Leading with your WHY means doing this in reverse.

Identify your goal or outcome first, then consider the best way to put your values and strengths to work to make big things happen.

2. FIND YOUR HIVE

Look around. Who have you chosen to surround yourself with? It's likely you're drawn to others with similar ideals. Being a part of a community with shared principles reinforces what you stand for. It strengthens your confidence. It provides a sense of well-being. It demonstrates you're a part of something bigger. It's a powerful reminder of how a group of like-minded individuals can make a difference when they come together. As a business owner, when you share your WHY with the world, you're making a conscious effort to connect with customers, supporters and employees who align with your purpose, invest in your brand, and value their relationship with you. This is your hive. Your WHY attracts your hive.

3. PLAN ON PURPOSE

Businesses typically lead with WHAT they do instead of WHY they do it—chances are you have too. Making this monumental shift in how you talk about your business, and doing it with confidence, calls for a solid communications plan. The good news is that you've already completed key components of your plan. You've developed your Pitch on Purpose, WHY Statement and Whyography, which are foundational for your purpose-driven brand. Incorporate these into your company's communications strategies and continue to build on your WHY.

WALK INSIDE YOUR STORY AND OWN IT.

BRENÉ BROWN

EPILOGUE

OWNING YOUR STORY

"Your position is being eliminated," my new boss's boss, who was sitting across from my desk, said briskly.

Suddenly I couldn't move. I could hear him speaking, but I couldn't open my mouth to respond. It was probably for the best. As he spoke about reorganization and implementing a vertical management structure, only curse words came to mind. I knew exactly what was happening. The job title was changing. The salary was shrinking. The role was being filled by someone with less experience. Probably someone on my team. It wasn't really the position that was being eliminated; it was me.

Up until that day, I was certain I had arrived. Before I turned 30, I had already met the professional goals I planned for myself. I had set my sights on working in a director-level position at a respected advertising agency or media outlet. And there I was, leading the marketing department for a radio station in the city that birthed my favorite musician of all time—Prince—whom I imagined meeting one day.

I was good at my job. No, I was *great* at it. I had an office in a renovated historical warehouse just one block away from First Avenue, the famous nightclub where the movie "Purple Rain" was filmed. One entire wall of my office was glass. It overlooked the building's atrium, which featured a full-size glider plane suspended from the ceiling. The other walls were covered with artwork from recording artists and record companies. The shelf above my desk displayed VIP badges from concerts and meet-and-greets along with framed photos capturing dozens of memories. There were premieres and parties and press events galore.

I'd spent the bulk of my 20s at that radio station—seven years in total. And yet there I was, in my beautiful office, in a job I never imagined leaving, the recipient of a textbook layoff executed the exact same way I'd been taught by the higher-ups to sack members of my own staff.

In the weeks leading up to my layoff, a lot had changed. There were seven radio stations under the same corporate umbrella in Minnesota. They were being run by two general managers in two different buildings. A market manager—my boss's boss—was put in place to lead marketing and programming for all seven stations. He had recently selected one marketing director under each roof to oversee marketing for the radio stations in their building. My counterpart at the Top 40 station was that person in our building, and he was now my new boss.

I was professional with my new boss, even before he was my boss, but we were far from friends. Rumor had it he was behind several anonymous and highly inappropriate posts about me on a radio industry message board. Higher-ups cautioned staff to stay off the message boards but didn't investigate who was behind the harassment. When the latest reporting structure was announced, I asked my new boss's boss about the possibility of reporting to the other marketing director in town. He denied my request based on proximity—I needed to report to someone in my building.

I was certain my new boss was to blame for this sudden change in my employment status. I labeled it a "firing disguised as a layoff," and I couldn't stop talking about it. Close friends patiently listened to me fume about it for the next few days. A week or so later, as a former co-worker and I were having lunch, she interrupted my rant about how it was going to be impossible to find a new job when I'd been fired from my last job. She gave me a dose of tough love.

"You were laid off, not fired," she said firmly. "Your personnel file says you were laid off. You're going to tell prospective employers you were laid off. Anyone who verifies your employment will be told you were laid off. You'll have a new job in no time."

Two weeks after the layoff, I had an interview at another radio station and got a job offer the same day. A few months after that, the general manager of a brand-new hip-hop radio station called to recruit me and offered me a job over the phone. My career moved forward. The world kept spinning. I finally met Prince. But I was stuck. I had been wronged. And for years, the people closest to me heard on repeat the version of the story where I was the victim of my former boss's devious scheme to ruin my career. I couldn't let it go.

Then, five years later I was laid off again—this time by the general manager who'd recruited me. It still sucked. The difference this time was that I realized it wasn't me that had been eliminated; it was my position. There were massive layoffs happening in the telecommunications industry on a regular basis. Layoffs happen in every industry, every day in America. It's just a fact of business.

My epiphany was this: Rather than owning my story, my story had owned me. The version I'd been telling did not honor my journey at all. It made my former boss a co-star when he was barely a walk-on. I was so focused on what I'd lost that I couldn't see what I had gained in the process. Once the perceived status and job perks had been stripped away, I realized the industry wasn't the best fit for me. Something good could come from it. I could leverage my connections and my behind-the-scenes media expertise to benefit mission-driven organizations—to do work that fueled my purpose. Rather than working at the mercy of a big corporation, I could do it on my own terms as a business owner. So that's exactly what I did.

Today, I fully own my story. All of it. Even the messy parts. The truth is, I may not have left the radio industry if I hadn't been laid off. I may not have left the museum world if I wasn't nudged. I may not have realized the extent to which women continue to be denied opportunities to thrive if I hadn't seen it with my own two eyes. It's all part of my journey, and there's no shame in any of it. What I've learned, like countless others before me, is that it takes a whole lot of living—from extreme joy to total heartbreak and everything in between—before the path that's meant for you starts to become clear. When it does, and you devote your life to your purpose, your heart will overflow. It will change your life. And, in turn, you will change the lives of others.

ACKNOWLEDGMENTS

Many thanks to the amazing women who believed in my seed of an idea, helped bring the Whyography program to life, continue to make it possible, and share a passion for championing women in business— Tracy Pleschourt, Allison Wyeth, Carlye Rooney, Katie Kosseff, Stef Tschida, Anna Befort, Jane Oslund, Barb Gehlen and Kate Hopper.

To the thousands of female business founders who are defying odds, launching and growing thriving businesses, and confidently sharing their stories with the world—you are the fuel that keeps me moving forward each day.

And to my partner in life, Matthew Howie, thank you for teaching me the definition of perseverance and for showing me that dreams have no expiration date. Thank you for encouraging me to keep writing, reminding me to look at sunsets and stars and flowers, and providing the inspiration for so much of what I write about.

ABOUT THE AUTHOR

Chris Olsen is a strategic storyteller who has devoted her career to connecting individuals and organizations using the power of words, images and experiences. After more than a decade working in broadcast media, Chris launched a communications consultancy and began leveraging her behind-the-scenes media expertise to benefit small businesses and nonprofit organizations.

Through her work as a consultant, Chris realized her WHY—to support female-identifying business owners and authors in confidently communicating their purpose and impact, setting them up for success. She created Publish Her and Publish Her Story as platforms for doing so.

A native of Minneapolis, Minnesota, Chris now enjoys life in the country surrounded by organic veggie gardens and her art teacher partner's overflowing pottery studio. She spends her free time writing and volunteering as a youth mentor for Big Brothers Big Sisters.

www.ingramcontent.com/pod-product-compliance
Lightning Source LLC
Chambersburg PA
CBHW080838120626
46553CB00009B/2485